The Write Way

Becoming a Successful Writer

Susan Crossman

Manor House

Library and Archives Canada Cataloguing in Publication

Crossman, Susan, author
   The write way : becoming a successful writer
/ Susan Crossman.

  ISBN 978-1-897453-40-7 (pbk.)

     1. English language--Rhetoric--Handbooks, manuals, etc.
I. Title.

PE1408.C76 2013   808'.0427   C2013-906047-2

Printed and bound in Canada

First Edition.

144 pages.

Cover design: Donovan Davie and Michael Davie
Cover art: Shutterstock

Published October 15, 2013
Manor House Publishing Inc.
www.manor-house.biz 905-648-2193

We gratefully acknowledge the financial support of the
Government of Canada through Book Fund Canada, Dept. of
Canadian Heritage.

For my mother, Gertrude Crossman, in whom a love of words has always flourished

Acknowledgements

How do I ever include every single being on the planet who has had a hand in my development as a writer and in the development of the material presented here in this book? I could start with my parents, both of whom loved to read, and I could follow that vote of gratitude with huge thanks to my public and high school teachers, who drilled into me the ABCs of stringing sentences. Grammar and spelling were important subjects when I was growing up and I deeply regret they're not a priority in our school systems today.

Although there are many valiant teachers out there straining to pack strong language skills into a curriculum already full to the brim with topics they hold their nose and teach, I herewith launch a plea to parents to insist your children learn proper grammar. It will save them a huge amount of money if they ever write a book and need an editor like me to correct it into readable format for them. And it will give them career advantages they might not otherwise enjoy. We know that literacy relates directly to economic wealth. It's a key life skill.

I appreciate my university professors who were sticklers for detail and I appreciate all the mentors who guided me along in my career, and who loved a good story, well and accurately told, as much as I did: Bruce Mechbach, Tony Bembridge, John McHugh, Ann Marie Montgomery, Rick Winchell, Pat Folliott and Rob Morgan. I'll add to that list Brian Henry, who taught me much about creative writing, and the writers who kept me enchanted through many a secret hour spent hiding under the covers with a flashlight and a sense of awe: Lucy Maud Montgomery, Louisa May Alcott, the Brontes, every single one, and, later in life, Stephen Leacock, Charles Dickens, Mark Twain, George

Eliot and Jane Austen... to name but a very few of my writing mentors, heroes and heroines.

I appreciate my children, Heather, Michael and Michelle, whose support of my somewhat unpredictable writing career has felt like the only support I've had, at times.

Leah Roberts deserves special mention here. Her cheerful assistance, eye for detail, positive energy and overall brilliance supplement a can-do attitude that never ceases to fill me with gratitude. As a member of my business team and my family, she is one of the rare people on this Earth who bring a sense of hope and inspiration everywhere she turns.

To Michael Davie, CEO of Manor House Publishing, I give great thanks for continuing to honour me with his voice of encouragement and confidence in my abilities as a writer. I am blessed indeed to work with a publisher whose attention to detail and devotion to quality even exceeds my own and I appreciate his dedication to the publishing industry in general and his authors in particular.

There are many missing from this list and I hope you know who you are and feel the grace of appreciation I will continually send your way. In closing, I'd like to say thank you to the former CEO of Franklin-Covey, Hyrum Smith. I heard him speak in Dallas, Texas, recently, and he said the words that should galvanize all of us into taking action to improve our ability to communicate with words: "You cannot think," he said, "any deeper than your vocabulary will allow."

With good wishes for expansion on all fronts,

Susan Crossman

"All readers come to fiction as willing accomplices to your lies. Such is the basic goodwill contract made the moment we pick up a work of fiction."
—Steve Almond

There is a crack in everything – that's how the light gets in
– Leonard Cohen

"If a nation loses its storytellers, it loses its childhood."
—Peter Handke

"Know your literary tradition, savor it, steal from it, but when you sit down to write, forget about worshiping greatness and fetishizing masterpieces."
—Allegra Goodman

"I do not over-intellectualize the production process. I try to keep it simple: Tell the damned story."
—Tom Clancy

"A scrupulous writer, in every sentence that he writes, will ask himself at least four questions, thus: 1. What am I trying to say? 2. What words will express it? 3. What image or idiom will make it clearer? 4. Is this image fresh enough to have an effect?"
— George Orwell

Table of Contents

One of the glories of English simplicity is the possibility of using the same word as noun and verb.
– **Edward Sapir**

I merely took the energy it takes to pout and wrote some blues.
– **Duke Ellington**

Language is wine upon the lips.
– **Virginia Woolf**

The person born with a talent they are meant to use will find their greatest happiness in using it."
– **Johann Wolfgang von Goethe**

The first step ... to controlling your world is to control your culture. To model and demonstrate the kind of world you demand to live in. To write the books. Make the music. Shoot the films. Paint the art.
— **Chuck Palahniuk**

Writing and reading decrease our sense of isolation. They deepen and widen and expand our sense of life: they feed the soul. When writers make us shake our heads with the exactness of their prose and their truths, and even make us laugh about ourselves or life, our buoyancy is restored. We are given a shot at dancing with, or at least clapping along with, the absurdity of life, instead of being squashed by it over and over again.
— **Anne Lamott**

Foreword

Susan Crossman has created one of the most comprehensive books on writing ever written. Whether you're writing a business report, an essay or a full-length novel, Crossman offers invaluable advice on making the process move more smoothly and efficiently. She also provides insightful tips on avoiding writer's block. If you want to be a truly effective and successful writer, this is the book you need.

From my personal experience as a writer, I've found that before sitting down with a coffee in a classic writer's pose to start writing and waiting impatiently for ideas to arrive, it really helps to first walk around collecting my thoughts , think about what I want to write about and run the ideas and phrases through my mind.

Doing that exercise means that when I do sit down to start writing, I've already written a lot of it in my head. It then becomes a matter of typing out those thoughts; then adding details and expanding on what you wrote in my head – then repeating this process.

Susan Crossman covers the benefits of going for a walk in good detail further along in a book that I wish had been released back when I first explored the fascinating craft of writing – her book is literally filled with helpful advice and tips for maximum efficiency and organization of thoughts and content.

I've also found that jotting quick notes of thoughts, phrases down here and there as they come to you throughout the day can also help as they give you a lot of points/content to include when you do get a chance to write.

As well, leaving a small bit unwritten when you're ready for a break leaves you with something you can immediately add and expand upon when you do return, kick-starting the resumption of writing and leading to more thoughts and ideas more easily to stop writer's block.

All of this too is also addressed in good detail and with full discussion in Susan Crossman's remarkable book on engaging and effective writing.

This is truly solid, expert advice from a professional writer and author of several critically acclaimed books. From tips on overcoming writer's block and engaging your audience to focusing on specific markets, Susan Crossman delivers insightful commentary that will help anyone become a more efficient, effective and successful writer.

Crossman's book is of tremendous benefit to business writers – and to anyone crafting works of fiction and non-fiction – a must-read!

– **Michael B. Davie**, author *Winning Ways*

Introduction:

I meet a lot of people in the course of an average week and I always divulge my occupation with a mixture of sweet pride and delight. I consider writing important work, and whether I am creating web content for one client or editing a book manuscript for another, I get to feel the satisfaction that comes from being of service. And it's such a fun job!

I started my professional writing career in 1982 and although I've taken time off for births, deaths, and a variety of other emergencies, I have worked hard and trained almost continuously for more than 30 years. I've worked in journalism, government and corporate communications, PR and marketing. I have an M.A. in English and an M.Ed. I'm a General and a Master Practitioner of NLP and I'm trained in both the Enneagram system of personality profiling and the DISC. I speak five languages (three well) and I am a certified Awakening Coach. Language is my stock in trade but it's also my life's calling.

Not everyone has taken that path. I'm all too aware that English grammar is not drilled into the heads of young people now the way it was when I was a scrawny 10-year-old pondering the difference between an indirect object and a subject completion. There are an awful lot of rules in English grammar and it's not everybody's bag of chips.

But I'm convinced that language facility in general, and English grammar in particular, can contribute much to success in life.

Express yourself well and convincingly, and you open the doors to all manner of important life transactions: more customers for your business, better relationships with friends and colleagues, support for a cause you value, receipt of that job you wanted…whatever you want is yours if you can win the attention and support of other people. The tool we all use to do that is language. So of course, the better we use that tool, the greater our results will be on all fronts.

And while I believe that literacy is a major the key to financial success on an individual basis, Statistics Canada has been busy pointing out that a population's literacy skills have a bearing on how well that country performs economically as well. Canada's labour market — and that of many other developed countries — has evolved from being based primarily on manufacturing and agriculture to one that emphasizes services. This change has engendered rising skill requirements and there a concern as to whether or not literacy skills in this country have changed apace. We operate in a globalized information economy now: can we meet that challenge?

According to the Conference Board of Canada, the literacy skills of 40 per cent of Canadian adults are too low to be fully competent in most jobs in our modern economy. The International Adult Literacy Survey, from which this information was derived, determined that in the United States that figure was an even more disturbing 48 per cent, and it has apparently risen to 53 per cent in the years since that study was completed.

The Conference Board further notes that one-quarter of all adults in the Canadian labour force are only marginally literate, which obviously has serious repercussions on their ability to understand and follow written directions. Improving the literacy skills of this group would deliver significant positive results for employers, in terms of productivity, innovation and bottom line results. The employees themselves would benefit from higher earnings, better work performance and better quality of life overall.

The ability to communicate clearly is obviously an advantage for businesses. And individuals. And that's partly why I wrote this book: I wanted to share some of what I've learned over the past three decades as a writer so other people can sharpen their skills as well.

There are reams of information available online about writing and there are many excellent books that walk the same path. Every writer brings a dash of their own personality into their insights and so you will find this book reflects the approach I tend to take in the work I do.

This is by no means an exhaustive book, but I rather think of it as something of a companion, an encouraging friend to take along on your own writing journey — to give you a few pointers, and perhaps a little nudge, as you find your way to the writer you are becoming.

We all recognize that writing is a creative process but we also tend to think of the physical process of writing as a mechanical skill that takes good grammar and a decent vocabulary and somehow blends them all together to create clear communication.

That's not a bad start but decades of experience have taught me that writing with impact is much more complex.

This book provides tips on:

- How to structure your written work

- Business writing advice

- Marketing and writing

- How to write with style

- How to engage an audience

- Avoiding and overcoming writer's block

Writing for key markets and marketing your writing in a highly effective manner

I hope it will help you write with more clarity and conviction and I also hope that it will make the task of writing more enjoyable.

And I wish you well! If this companion proves to be a positive addition to your bookshelf, drop me a line and let me know! If there is other material you would like to see covered in a future book, tell me that as well. And if you feel I can help you get your story out in the world, either as a writer, an editor, a speaker or a coach, by all means, get in touch at susan@crossmancommunications.com.

Best wishes for many successful writing adventures,

Susan Crossman

If there's a book that you want to read, but it hasn't been written yet, then you must write it.
— **Toni Morrison**

The first draft of anything is shit.
— **Ernest Hemingway**

Writers live twice.
—**Natalie Goldberg**

Our admiration of fine writing will always be in proportion to its real difficulty and its apparent ease.
– **Charles Caleb Colton**

I look for ambiguity when I'm writing because life is ambiguous.
– **Keith Richards**

Writing is easy: All you do is sit staring at a blank sheet of paper until drops of blood form on your forehead.
– **Gene Fowler**

A person is a fool to become a writer. His only compensation is absolute freedom. He has no master except his own soul, and that, I am sure, is why he does it
— **Roald Dahl**

The only way you can write the truth is to assume that what you set down will never be read. Not by any other person, and not even by yourself at some later date. Otherwise you begin excusing yourself. You must see the writing as emerging like a long scroll of ink from the index finger of your right hand; you must see your left hand erasing it.
— **Margaret Atwood**

I think writing really helps you heal yourself. I think if you write long enough, you will be a healthy person. That is, if you write what you need to write, as opposed to what will make money, or what will make fame.
– **Alice Walker**

I am never going to have anything more to do with politics or politicians. When this war is over I shall confine myself entirely to writing and painting.
– **Winston Churchill**

Writing is a form of therapy; sometimes I wonder how all those who do not write, compose or paint can manage to escape the madness, melancholia, the panic and fear which is inherent in a human situation.
– **Graham Greene**

I learned never to empty the well of my writing, but always to stop when there was still something there in the deep part of the well, and let it refill at night from the springs that fed it.
– **Ernest Hemingway**

Chapter One: Structure and Writing with Impact

One of the most important components of writing well is good organization. Before you can even hope to inform or influence a reader, you absolutely must have an intelligent plan that focuses your thinking and guides your writing.

I use a simple five-step kick-start for almost every document I write. Here it is:

1. Set your goals:

You need to start with a clear idea of what you want this piece to do for you. Do you want it to confirm your standing as an expert, influence readers to take action, inform people about something important or simply give yourself a chance to vent?

2. Know your audience:

Your audience information will dictate the complexity of language needed, the type and amount of detail required and the overall voice necessary to reach your audience. Miss this piece and you blow your chance to connect.

3. Collect your facts:

Writer's Block is often caused by a lack of pertinent information so whenever I hit that intellectual brick wall I generally head out and do more research.

Filtering out irrelevant material is much easier than trying to invent details you should already have, and it gives you the luxury of being selective about the information you include.

4. Organize your information well:

Once you have corralled all the facts, what do you do with them? I organize them into four main categories that deal with:

- Why my topic is important

- What it involves

- How it works and

- What the future implications are

I tack on a package of introductory information and a collection of conclusions and I'm good to go.

5. Check for what's missing:

It's easy to get lost in detail but you also need to step back from all that glorious information and ask yourself what you've left out.

You might have overlooked something stunningly basic and it's a lot easier to find that out before you start writing than to be called on the carpet for the omission at a later date.

Once you've done all this preliminary work you end up with a document that practically writes itself.

So let's look at each one of these steps in more detail:

Step One: You Need a Goal

Taking a moment to get a solid idea of the purpose of your document keeps your writing from wandering into irrelevant territory that might confuse or bore your audience. It also keeps you focused and selective, which gives your work much more impact.

Most business communication falls into one of four categories and your goal for most writing projects will likely be to:

1. Explain a situation

2. Analyze an issue

3. Promote a product or service or

4. Inspire a reaction

If you're a writing keener and want to take it to another level entirely, bear this in mind: while your document will do one of the above it should also do all three of the following:

- Influence your audience

- Support one or more goal and

- Deepen key relationships

Before I start to write anything official, I type a little note to myself that reads like this:

"The purpose of this document is to (state purpose).

"I want to influence my audience to (add answer).

"I need to make sure the following business goals are addressed (list them).

"I want to inspire my audience to (elaborate).

Once I have my direction clear I can be more discerning about the development of the rest of my article and I don't waste a second dithering. That makes me efficient and decisive and really adds to my enjoyment of the process of writing.

It's not always as easy as 1,2,3 --but writing doesn't have to be a misery.

Step Two: Understand Your Audience.

This is a big one.

The success of efforts to promote a product, service, program or opinion are almost entirely dependent upon how well you connect with your audience.

That means you need to know as much as possible about who they are, what they like and dislike, how they react to different values and ideas and what motivates them to act.

Every word you write about your business or service needs to correspond with your audience's model of the world so you can develop the kind of rapport that invites trust.

Honesty is key and you need to be authentic in your determination to provide a quality product or service that truly meets an existing need in an existing audience. Finding that audience and speaking directly to them is what marketing is all about.

If there is a disconnect between what you offer and what your audience wants, then you have two choices:

1. Change your product, service or program so that it corresponds more closely to audience demand or

2. Find a different audience – one that is more suited to what you offer.

Knowing your audience means gathering insights related to their age, marital staus, education, occupation, income level, family situation, interests and pursuits, geographic location, biggest challenges and greatest joys.

When you start writing, this information will help you select words, phrases, metaphors and imagery that will resonate with your readers.

It will also help you position different aspects of your offering (the "features") as specific benefits that will improve readers' lives in fundamental ways.

Remember that promotional documents are not about what YOU feel is great about your product or service – they're about what your audience needs, wants and cares about. Your value lies in solving problems for them.

Step Three: Collect Your Facts

Information for most types of business writing tends to come from a variety of resources: interviews, reports and online resource material are most common.

You need to be a "Detail Drone" at this part of the process because it's often a tiny piece of innocuous information that can elevate your article to new heights. For example, I once wrote a promotional article about a retirement home manager, a large man with uncommonly large hands. He had a great laugh and a ready smile, and all of the expected qualifications for running a retirement home with integrity. But his hands became the anchor for the piece and the article ultimately reflected the fact that residents could rest assured that with this man in charge, they were "in very good hands."

If I had not been filtering for small details, I would have missed that opportunity.

Not all details are going to be relevant and I'll caution that not all writers like working with detail – some of us are more comfortable with "big picture" topics.

But your goal at this stage is to collect everything you can get your hands on so you can work towards the writing stage, where the more elegant craftsmanship takes place.

Step Four: Organize Your Information

So you've determined the purpose of your document, put some thought into who your audience is, gathered far more information than you can humanly use and consumed way too much coffee in the vain effort to forestall information overload.

The file facing you is a long dreary litany of unrelated and quite scrambled information and it is sitting there daring you to do something with it.

You think perhaps it is time to answer some emails or call your mother. This is typical writer behavior so you are in good shape for the next stage of writing, which is to organize your information.

This is not for the faint of heart but I have a dandy little template for wrangling all that information into a form that anybody can use, and it's one that will make instant sense to your audience. The information is based on the work of Dr. Bernice McCarthy, a leading expert on learning who did some amazing work on determining how people process and retain information.

So let's just dive in:

You need four headings: Why? What? How? and So What?

Starting at the top of your file, go through all of your information and move any information that explains "why" your topic is important to a spot under the "Why" heading. When that's done, do the same thing for information that explains "What" your topic or program is and next, "How" it works.

If this is an original document you may need to throw in some point-form explanations of your own to round out the subject matter in each of these three areas. When all that's done, you can tackle the "So What" area, which is really just a summary of why anybody should care – what is the "big dream" your project makes possible or what new potential does it unlock in the world?

If your material neglects to provide satisfactory details, add in the ones you know yourself to be true (with references if necessary).

You will probably be staring at a passel of leftover information that doesn't seem to belong anywhere.

Check through it again just to be sure none of it answers "Why, What, How or So What" and then take one more look to see if it contains any nuggets of information that might make either a great introduction or a fabulous conclusion.

You need both, so if the existing material doesn't help you out, you'll need to develop them yourself.

That means you need to make a new heading just above the "Why" heading, and it will read "Introduction."

Follow this with another new heading just below the "So What" heading, which will read "Conclusion."

Add in all the information you think applies to these categories and go grab another coffee.

Step Five: Check for What's Missing

Some people are surprised to hear that writing with impact requires a great deal of organization and I think that word "writer" is to blame. It is a highly romantic word. It conjures a soft-focus vision of a dreamy-eyed youth shut away in a cluttered attic room with nothing but a blotty pen and a tattered notebook for company.

Organization is not romantic.

The previous step took readers through the messy but crucial process of organizing information into four key areas (Why, What, How and So What?).

We tacked on a chunk of introductory information and a chunk of concluding information. Before we start knitting all that information into the glorious creation of a proper document, however, we have to step back and check for what's missing.

It sounds pretty simple but plenty of people neglect this piece. We know from studies in psychology that some people are highly motivated to solve problems – these people enjoy looking for what's missing from their information.

Other people are motivated to achieve goals. These people will likely find the process of checking for what's missing to be highly tedious. And for pity's sake, we haven't even started the "actual" writing!

Neither tendency is wrong – but if you are highly goal-oriented you may need to force yourself to complete this task. And let's face it, if you have left out an important fact, argument or shade of meaning it's a lot easier to find out before you start writing than to regret the omission at a later date.

Once you have all the information you need – and it's all nicely organized – you can then start crafting sentences to tie it all together.

At that point in my five-step process for structuring your writing, your document will practically write itself and your job is to then focus on the style issues that will make the piece coherent and expressive.

I find that writing a document this way is something like sculpting a great work of art from a large block of wood.

You carefully chip and scrape away the material you don't need and mould the remainder according to your vision of what the piece should be like; eventually the final shape emerges.

The floor will be littered with messy chips of unused verbiage but the document itself will be something graceful and articulate and, actually, maybe there is something a little romantic in that concept.

But the goal is to communicate clearly, and that can only happen if you're well organized and focused on ensuring your audience understands what you have to say.

Chapter Two: Writing with Style

Although structure is a fundamental component of good writing, most people consider it to be only slightly more interesting than leaf lettuce and many people find this next block of lessons in my personal writing curriculum much more to their taste. These lessons deal with **Style**.

The word "style" stems from the Latin "stilus," a word originally used to denote a writing implement that was used to scratch messages on wax tablets. Today the word style might refer to a way of dressing or living, and in the context of writing, it denotes a way of writing.

The internet is rife with definitions of what "writing style" actually means. And many news organizations maintain their own style guides that set out exactly how language is to be used by reporting staff. Writers are expected to learn their employer's style conventions and editors are expected to be vigilant in ensuring there are no deviations.

The Canadian Press Stylebook and the Chicago Manual of Style are two authoritative sources used in North America and there are many others out there as well.

My own favorite style guide is the irresistible "Manual of Style," written by William Strunk Jr., and it's available on www.bartleby.com, itself a rich miscellany of writing resources.

For the purposes of this series, however, I'm going to differentiate between writing to conform to a specific style and writing with style.

We've all encountered written documentation that is a chore to read. It might get the point across and it might contain relevant information. But it is clunky and utterly lacking in fluidity; it probably doesn't make consistent sense and it has no impact. This ultimately reflects poorly on the originating organization and it is bad for business; from a reputation perspective, corporate writing must be strong.

It can take years of consistent effort to learn how to write smoothly, but as as writers become more confident in their writing, they inevitably develop their own personal style and a voice that defines them and their work.

A writer's natural inclinations might have to be somewhat repressed in order to align with a corporate image and style, but gracefulness can still reign regardless.

In my experience, I've found that graceful, stylish writing requires:

Grammatical accuracy – with full attention paid, for example, to correct tenses, verb conjugation, and spelling.

Smooth linkages between sentences and paragraphs within the document.

3. **Lively word choice** that brings color, variety, creativity and appropriate pacing to the document.

4. **Good depth** created by the use of analogies, metaphors and appropriate mood (subjunctive, imperative and indicative for you grammar groupies!) and

5. **Strong editing** – delete unnecessary words!

Step One for Writing with Style: Grammatical Accuracy

This publication focuses on improving your writing style as painlessly as possible - but it's a good idea to keep in mind that good writing is not always completely painless: it often involves the selection, examination, dismissal, replacement, repositioning and deletion of what could amount to hundreds, if not thousands, of innocent words.

It can take hours of writing and rewriting to get it all just perfect. And even then it's possible someone else might be able to find ways to improve the text. We give it our best shot, though, and having organized our information well, we can then segue into the fascinating area of writing with style.

At first blush, grammar might not seem like an important part of style - but it's impossible to write delightfully without it. In the context of business, if you mess up your tenses or verb conjugations, you risk confusing your reader; worse still, you will sound unprofessional. Good grammar leads directly to credibility and although that's changing with texting, tweeting and our increasing reliance on video messages, writing with proper grammar is still a competitive advantage.

This is a subject that frightens many people, either because they didn't learn it properly in public school or because grammar was out of fashion when they passed through. But there is nothing magic about grammar – it's simply a set of rules and conventions about how to build sentences that are logical, straightforward and easy to understand. Each rule or convention is simple to learn and easy to follow – but you do have to invest whatever time is necessary to develop a strong competency in the subject.

Here are some ways you might do that:

1. Juvenile as it sounds, I often recommend people buy a set of public school grammar exercise books (Grade One to Grade Eight) and work their way through them one lesson at a time. This is an old-fashioned form of information delivery and it works.

2. Visit an English-as-a-Second-Language website - About.com offers some excellent resources - and you can work your way through the lesson plans and online tests, building your competency at your own speed.

3. Read one paragraph of the "Manual of Style" by William Strunk Jr. every day. Absorb the wisdom each section imparts and then practice what you've learned. I like my hardcopy version but you can also find it on bartleby.com.

4. Visit your local Literacy Council (real or virtual locations) and find out if you are a candidate for a literacy training program.

5. Read. But don't just read to consume the words, read to observe how the writer put the words together.

Polishing your grammar may seem dreary but it's one of the easiest ways to improve your writing style.

Step Two for Writing with Style: Linkages

Have you ever noticed that some written documents seem to flow more smoothly than others? While there are a number of factors at work, one of the most important is the strength of the writer's linkages.

I define a linkage as the small piece of geography that steers the ending of one sentence or paragraph into the beginning of the next one. You want that nexus point to be as natural, normal and unobtrusive as possible – in a way, you want to turn the spaces between your sentences and paragraphs into tiny little virtual bridges your readers can easily cross.

I use a number of techniques to do this and here are some of my favourites:

1. **Conjunctions.** A conjunction is a word that joins two parts of a sentence and they're invaluable! There are many conjunctions available to us but here are a few you probably already know: After, Although, As, As long as, As soon as, Because, Before, If , Since, Than, Unless, Until, Whenever, and While.

While conjunctions are useful in the middle of a sentence, they are just as helpful for starting a new sentence or paragraph. As long as you do so as gracefully as possible. Although some grammarians might quibble with the idea, I find that whenever I'm stuck for a "bridge" to my next sentence or paragraph, I will often pull out a conjunction and go from there. (Just as I've done in this paragraph.)

2. **Refer to a previous thought.** Conjunctions aren't always the perfect way to start a new paragraph, however, and

sometimes it's helpful to take an idea from a previous paragraph and use it as a springboard to catapult readers towards a new topic. (As I've just done here.) Readers won't give it a second thought.

3. **Or will they?** Asking questions is also a good way to move the document into new territory.

4. **Use interpretive comments.** They're easy and authoritative, for example: "What that means is that ..." or "At first blush that might sound confusing but...."

5. **Play with time.** Most people tend to have either a past or a future orientation and it's rare to find an individual who is comfortable with both. That being said, we all understand both concepts and I capitalize on this understanding of time as a "flow" when I'm writing. For example, I might start a sentence or paragraph by saying "While that might have been true in the past, these days things are changing." Or "New ideas like that are great but they haven't always created a proven track record.

6. **Miscellaneous helper phrases.** I have a few stock phrases that I also keep on hand for those moments of terror when my mind goes blank and I can't think of what to say next. To help smooth out your own linkages, try one of these and see if it works for you:

In the meantime,

Here's the thing:

For the record,

Once people have …

The opportunities are …

It may take a while to get the hang of using all these different techniques for linking different parts of your paragraph or document but they've all worked for me at various times in the past and I'm always on the lookout for more.

Step Three: Use Lively Words!

While linkages are important, Step Three in my lessons for Writing with Style deals with something that is probably a little more fun, and that is the importance of **liveliness in writing**. Lively word choice keeps people interested in what they're reading and complements the solid foundation you've laid by embellishing it. I'm not talking about anything grandiose or outlandish — just the little touches that add a whisper of surprise or interest. Like the word "whisper," for example.

This is not as easy as it sounds. Most of us have a standard range of words that we insert into our documents almost by rote, and expanding that range requires us to expand our vocabulary. That almost always involves the use of a dictionary or a thesaurus, which requires more effort and more time. The Oxford English Dictionary (OED) Online has a great "word of the day" service that I find is a painless way to make friends with words I might not ordinarily encounter. Here's the link: http://www.oed.com/.

And I use my thesaurus often. Although the one that comes with Word is reasonably good, I still resort to my dog-eared copy of Roget's Thesaurus from time to time. Mine has a complicated numbering system that I'm sure was set up by a mathematician, but it is an absolutely brilliant way to explore my native tongue. A writer's style is something like a signature and as you develop your style, you find that your word choice is reflective of your outlook. This can get stale.

You'll want to round out what you offer readers by taking chances every now and then so you can bring variety and color to your work. Even if what you're writing is a thoroughly standard business report, a little variety will help engage your audience and keep people reading. Choose boring words and, yes, you'll bore your audience. None of us pays superb attention when we're bored. You want to make it easy for your audience to embrace your topic!

Step Four for Writing with Style: Depth

Much as we sometimes gloss over the issue of writing in businesses these days, there is simply no arguing with the fact that strong writing supports the bottom line.

While many factors affect a person's ability to use the written word to communicate powerfully, I enjoy talking about style because it speaks to our individuality. By depth I mean careful use of analogies, metaphors, mood and the judicious use of questions. I look at depth in writing as similar to the seasoning in a great meal: you can get along without it, but you enjoy yourself much more when it's deftly applied.

Not everyone is adept at creating depth in writing and in truth it's one of the issues that I personally have had to work on in my own writing journey. I am by nature a very analytical person and although I have a creative streak a mile wide and 10 kilometres deep, I tend to default to the clinical in my writing. That's a safe place to be in the business world but it can get boring for readers. If my goal is to engage my audience and keep them leaning forward in their chairs to hear what else I have to say, then I need to stir things up a bit! I do that by layering in some depth. Here's how:

Analogies: An analogy is a comparison between two different things in order to highlight some point of similarity and clarify meaning.

Here's an example: Our short term memory is like the RAM on a computer – it's available for the here and now but not necessarily available for the long haul.

Metaphors: A metaphor expresses the unfamiliar in terms of the familiar – for example, when I mentioned above that depth in writing is similar to the seasoning in a great meal, I was speaking metaphorically.

Mood: In grammatical terms, mood refers to one of three forms of expression:

1. The indicative relates to a statement of fact: "My computer does not have enough RAM."

2. The imperative relates to a command: "Make sure you get a computer that has enough RAM!

3. The subjunctive more or less relates to statements that imply doubt about the truth or accuracy of a situation: "If I were a millionaire I would have many computers and unlimited RAM."

Questions: I use questions sparingly when I write and they are sometimes valuable from a promotional perspective.

Example: Are you interested in information about your industry that nobody else knows?

Some of these techniques require a writer to take a chance in their work and that's sometimes a scary prospect, so I recommend people play with these techniques in non-essential documents first. While not everybody connects "writing" with "fun," I think the key to doing it well lies in the concept of taking the leash off your creative side just enough to add some adventure to the mix.

Step Five for Writing with Style: Editing

Many businesspeople struggle a little with the task of writing with impact and although good writing might seem like a mysterious skill, I believe it's something almost anyone can develop. We are each on our own writing continuum and while some people are working to improve their grammar, others are trying to catch the knack of writing fluidly. There is no right or wrong in all this. It's a personal project.

Which brings us to the question of writing with style. It's quite personal as well and I've saved my favourite step for last: **Editing.** Contrary to what some people believe, great writing doesn't usually just flow magically and instantaneously from a writer's head, through their fingers and out onto the screen. It can be an agonizing process full of false starts and sentences that lead nowhere.

The trick to becoming a good writer lies in being able to take a messy, possibly incoherent tangle of sentences and trim them all into an orderly prism of language that is meaningful and effective. That's about editing.

When I switch from "Writing Mode" to "Editing Mode" I look for what's wrong in my document and then I fix it.

I'm checking for a number of different problems which might lie in the areas of: Spelling, Grammatical accuracy, Sentence structure, Flow, Freshness, Depth, Length, Goals I had initially set for the piece, Audience appeal, Factual accuracy, Overall organization and, finally, Missed opportunities for making my point.

While it can take me quite a while to finish editing a document, there comes a point when I have to say "enough's enough," and let the piece go. But I am usually reasonably happy with it by then.

If you find the task overwhelming, I suggest you find a supportive friend or colleague who loves working with words and who is willing to give your work an honest edit for you. Ask them to use the "track changes" function so you can learn from what they've done.

Alternatively, you can hire an editor like me to just take over and do it for you. Unfortunately there is no room for pandering to ego in editing. Having worked at a daily newspaper way back at the "Dawn of Time," I know how painful the experience of having someone else edit your work can be. But a great end result is what you're after, and if you need help, ask for it! There is no shame in wanting to improve.

A very good editor is almost a collaborator.
– **Ken Follett**

That element of surprise is what I look for when I am writing. It is my way of judging what I am doing – which is never an easy thing to do.
– **V. S. Naipaul**

If someone decides to be a musician now, it means because there is no hope of money at the end of it, it means they really want to be a musician. And if someone is writing now, there is no hope for money at the end of it.
– **Doug Coupland**

There are three rules for writing a novel. Unfortunately, no one knows what they are.
– **W. Somerset Maugham**

Life isn't about finding yourself. Life is about creating yourself.
— **George Bernard Shaw**

Books are the quietest and most constant of friends; they are the most accessible and wisest of counsellors, and the most patient of teachers.
— **Charles William Eliot**

Chapter Three: Writing for Audience Engagement

Writing well involves many fluid skill sets and distilling them all down into a concrete process risks eliminating the creative magic that can make a story really cook.

And although I respect the rules of the writing road, I also love the excitement of steering onto an unmarked trail and letting my imagination take the wheel. That applies even when I'm writing for business.

I think of an engaged reader as one who simply keeps on reading — not because they have to, but because they can't help themselves.

An engaged reader doesn't stop to think how nice the writing is – they're connecting directly with the material itself and floating along on the river of understanding the writer has created for them.

In corporate communications – or, indeed, in any field – that engagement is the key to ensuring our readers understand an issue, support an opinion or program, or take a desired action.

Here are my top five suggestions for writing to engage an audience:

1. **Tell people why your initiative is important.**

Never assume people will "get it" just because it makes sense to you. They need – and deserve – some solid information around why it's being introduced, why it will be helpful, and why they should support it.

2. **Show your audience you understand their pain.**
Referencing problems and other issues that relate to their key interests, for example, develops rapport with your audience. It is a form of respect.

3. **Add an emotional component.** Being human implies an emotional existence and a light reference to feelings acknowledges that we aren't just machines lined up waiting for quitting time. It doesn't have to be excessive to be effective – for example, I used the word "excitement" in the first paragraph of this chapter as part of an analogy about creativity to encourage interest and create depth.

4. **Reference experiences your audience will embrace.** A group of heli-skiers might understand the 9-to-5 world, for example, but they're probably going to be far more motivated by references to stretching the envelope of human existence in a "fresh powder" kind of way. So it is with an employee or stakeholder group: references to flex time or improvements to the company fitness centre might resonate more broadly than talk of a no-fall zone.

5. **Use language that incorporates different motivational precepts.** Bring words that will help your audience see, hear

and feel what you're talking about and show them you understand their need to deepen their business relationships, achieve their goals and control their environment. Where appropriate, show them how things will be exactly the same, and how they will be different, from what they're used to.

Help them understand the global vision at the heart of what you're describing, as well as the minute details that will make it work.

Step: The Importance of "Why?"

Being a writer is an awfully fun gig and I absolutely love what I do. The sheer bliss of stringing words together is like weaving magic on a page and there really is no thrill that can compare to doing that well.

But I've come to the point in life where I also like sharing that knowledge, and one of my other favourite things to do is to coach other writers in their own evolution.

Once a writer has learned how to structure their work well, and can write with a certain amount of style, I like to lead them through the most valuable set of writing skills for our competitive world and that is the basics of writing to engage an audience.

Engaging an audience is the most important step in motivating folks to understand your position, support your program or take a desired action.

Let's start with the **"Why"** issue.

Telling your audience why your topic is important shows them what the payoff is going to be and the more compelling you can make that, the better.

In a corporate communications setting, for example, your employees might want to know if it will help them do their job better or more efficiently, improve relationships with other people or between their department and another one, help them meet their objectives, or give them more control over their time or their area.

What's more, as Dr. McCarthy's work on the psychology of learning has shown, different people filter information differently. One of the most important sets of filters explores:

• why something is important

• what it is

• how it works OR

• what big dream it facilitates.

We might default to any of these areas at different times. But only one of them is our most important default filter in any given context.

As writers, we don't know which filter our readers are going to be using or when. We have to assume that incorporating each concept into our work is our only way of engaging everybody.

But there's a trick: it has to be done in the right order or we risk losing our audience.

The folks whose primary filtration system centres around "why" something is important need to be satisfied first. If you don't give them that information right off the top, they will tune you out and Bingo! you've lost the chance to inform or influence them.

It is certainly not difficult to include that information in your written work — you just have to remember to do it. You then follow with the what, the how and the "So what" information (which we covered in our chapter on Structure) and you're away to the races. But get that "Why" covered first!

Step Two: Understand your Reader's Pain

No matter where you are on the "writing continuum," you've no doubt encountered a situation where you needed to write an article or web page that grabbed audience attention and wouldn't let it go.

It's a stressful task for most of us — these things don't just write themselves.

And even if we know that the job requires creating rapport with our readers and engaging their interest, it's not always obvious what steps we need to take to get there.

Here's how I do it:

1. I tell people why my program or initiative is important.

2. I show them I understand their pain.

3. I add an emotional component.

4. I reference experiences my audience will embrace and

5. I use language that incorporates different motivational precepts.

We covered the "Why" component above and now let's look at the importance of showing your audience that you understand their pain.

My copywriting mentors have all dunned into me the importance of ensuring all my copy is phrased around my audience's experience, rather than my own.

Although it's something I feel I've always known, it can be very difficult to walk out of our own ego and focus entirely on the reader. I don't mean that unkindly – our ego is a determined piece of equipment that has a place in our personality. It just gets in the way of focusing on other people sometimes!

If you're a senior executive, or a corporate communicator, with some solid writing experience behind you, it might be worth remembering that much as you might command respect in your circle of influence, people generally aren't focused on you.

They're focused on their own lives. They're blurring through their daily chaos, and aren't especially concerned about what other folks tell them is exciting, interesting or important.

If you want to stop them in their tracks and pull them into your orbit, you need to tell them how what you're offering is going to make their lives easier, better, safer, more efficient, more interesting, more productive or more comfortable.

And of course, in order to decide which criteria to emphasize, you need to understand your readers' pain. What do your readers find difficult or discouraging?

If you aren't sure, ask them. And find out what you need to do to ease that pain. No empty promises, though – if you say you're going to help, then you really do need to help.

Step Three: Add Some Emotion!

There are many different skill sets involved in writing well and although I hear a lot of talk these days about how important good grammatical skills are, a 30-year career in writing has taught me that strong grammar is just the start.

The very best writers go way beyond grammar and structure their documents well, they have a smooth and sophisticated style, and when they write, people take note.

Their writing engages audience attention.

Part of that has to do with how gracefully they can add some emotional content to their writing.

Writing with emotion doesn't mean you're overwhelming people with feeling – indeed, in a business environment that is rarely, if ever, appropriate.

But if you want to make your work appealing and memorable, you want to mix in a few words that appeal to the emotional world of your readers.

Writing that's precise and crisp gets the point across nicely and that should always be our goal. But writing that hints at a life outside the corporate box reaches people where they really live. It confirms their humanity.

Here's an example: I recently wrote an article for a corporate client about the redevelopment of a municipal park situated on the outskirts of a bustling community.

Digging into the information available about the park online, I discovered that the park was said to be haunted. Obviously that's not a detail we're going to cover in a business article, but it led me to wonder what was on the land before the park got there and bingo! It turned out the property had been the site of a thriving village during the early years of the 1800s.

I tracked down an expert on local history and heard a world of interesting detail about the area's notable past. What a gold mine! The information allowed me to extend my article about the relocation of a bridge and the installation of new playground equipment into a story that hinted at the hopes and dreams of early settlers who came, and ultimately left, what was then a fairly remote area of Canada.

The park redevelopment was important for people living in the neighbourhood at the time; the knowledge about the community that preceded theirs imparted a sense of historical stability to the project. It captured people's imagination in a way statistics about machinery could not.

Try this in your work as well! It takes a little more effort but the payback is priceless.

Step Four: Share Experiences an Audience will Embrace

Engaging an audience can require a fairly sophisticated command of language and even competent writers sometimes struggle to create the level of interest that keeps an audience tuned in and turned on.

An important part of the process involves building rapport with your audience. Rapport is about establishing common ground with your readers by demonstrating that you understand their world and can bring value to it. It is the first step in developing a relationship, and this holds true in business as well as in personal situations.

There is no real mystery about developing rapport: when two people have a lot in common they get in sync with each other instinctively and rapport develops quickly.

But we don't always have that luxury when we're writing for business. You can initiate the process of developing rapport by taking a step into someone else's world and referencing issues, situations and concepts that are part of the landscape of their lives.

We've seen how you can do that in writing by showing your audience that you understand their pain (see Step Two above in this chapter).

But you can also extend your connection with your audience on a "big picture" level by lacing your writing with references your audience will understand.

For example: as I mentioned earlier, if you know that your audience includes a large number of people who enjoy heliskiing, you might want to use metaphors and similes that relate to fresh powder rather than library shelves.

Similarly, an audience of athletes might not connect deeply with language that incorporates the comforts of relaxing in front of the TV but they will perk up over the mention of pushing limits, straining muscles, improving performance, or hitting a personal best.

This is easier when your audience is relatively homogeneous and you know a lot about their interests. It's much harder when you don't know much about your audience or when its members have very little in common.

When relatively little information is available about my intended audience, I fall back on metaphors that have been proven to resonate with almost everyone on the planet. Most people will embrace writing that speaks of journeys, connections, transformation, balance, containers, resources or control. So at the very least, I know I can incorporate one or more of these concepts into my writing with a good chance of engaging my audience, whatever their specific interests are.

Step Five: Motivate Your Readers!

In my decades as a professional writer I have never been asked to write something where audience interest was optional and one of the ways I bring it all together is by using language that appeals to different segments of my audience.

For example, most people know that in any given audience we'll find some people who are kinesthetically oriented, some who are visual and some who are primarily audial in their behaviours and preferences. It's relatively easy to incorporate words and phrases that appeal to each of these three groups. But there are other sets of filters at work in an audience at any given time and getting comfortable with them will help you attract attention while avoiding problems in your appeal.

Here are some examples:

Toward and Away From: Some people take action if it means they are moving towards something they like or want, while others take action if it means they will move away from something they don't like or don't want. You can include both in your copy by using phrases like: "this will help you get the results you want while avoiding the problems you'd rather not encounter."

Global Vision and Specific Detail: Some people are big picture thinkers while others love the details. You can incorporate the interests of all by using phrases such as "this product is aimed at ensuring the global vision is served while still incorporating the important details that make everything work well."

Proactive and Reactive: Some folks make decisions quickly and like to take action immediately; others prefer to get as much information as they can first before they process it all very thoroughly. You can include both the proactive and reactive thinkers and doers in your copy by using phrases such as "If you know this is for you and you want to participate immediately, here's how..." and "On the other hand, if you feel you need time to think it over, here are some additional resources that might help you obtain all the information you need. Time is limited, however. This offer will end Friday."

Internal and External: Your audience will undoubtedly include people who don't like to be told what to do and who don't much care what other people think. Others will come to a decision about your product or service based on what other people think, and they will appreciate hearing what others have said on the topic. You can include both groups by using language such as: "We understand that this is an important issue and we know it's important for you to get as much information on the topic as possible before you decide...If you have any additional questions, please let us know. And "If you'd like to hear what other people have said about our product/service, please see our testimonials page for more information."

Those are obviously just general examples designed to give a broad sense of how motivational language patterns might work for you. There are many, many more ways to generate action in a diverse audience and they're all quite simple to learn.

Five Questions Every Author Should Ask about Working with an Editor:

I find that one of the many fun aspects of being a career writer is that I've had an opportunity to try my hand at a lot of different types of writing. I started out in journalism and over the past 30 years I have been fortunate in obtaining work in the areas of government and corporate communications, marketing, PR and creative writing.

Somewhere along the way I also walked into the world of editing as well.

Editing is very interesting and very detailed work and I love working with authors. I know from experience how thrilling it is to see a manuscript over which you have laboured become magically transformed into a book with your name on the front cover. And it's an honour to put my skill set to work on behalf of others.

If you've never had the opportunity to work with an editor before, however, the process can represent something of a "black box." This document is my way of peeling back the veils of mystery that shroud the book editing process so prospective authors can see why they might need an editor, what editing is, how it works and what the implications of having your work professionally edited are. Every editor works differently, so if you have a manuscript that you feel would benefit from a good edit, it's a good idea to ask a lot of questions and make sure you feel the person you are considering would be a good fit for your project.

Question #1 Why Do You Need an Editor?

We all get close to our subject matter and sometimes it's hard to determine if our work reads clearly and makes sense. And, too, in the drive to process reams of information and then write a brilliant piece on a short deadline, we sometimes inadvertently leave out pertinent information.

Sometimes we've made a silly grammatical error or written sentences that are a tad confusing. In any professional writing context, from journalism to marketing, there is an individual assigned to proof-read copy and safeguard the quality of that copy. This is no reflection on a writer's capability — it's just what smart businesses do to make sure that the written materials bearing their name are factually correct and linguistically sound.

The process protects and enhances reputations. When it comes to the world of book-writing, it's important that the manuscript reflects the author in the best light possible as well. An editor will catch mistakes, improve the prose, clarify what doesn't make sense and point out discrepancies in style and story line.

A good editor will polish your work so you are even more proud of what you have done than you ever thought possible. Editing falls into the category of necessity rather than luxury, regardless of whether you are going the self-publishing route or aiming to get your work published by a traditional publishing house.

One of the reasons my novel, "Shades of Teale," originally attracted the attention of my publisher, Manor House, was that I was able to tell them that it had been professionally edited. That showed I was serious about the quality of my work and the quality of my ideal readers' experiences.

Question #2 What Does Editing Involve?

Editing is a precise skill and different editors work differently. But overall, when an author engages an editor to work on their manuscript, they are handing their baby over to a stranger and trusting them to make the changes necessary to improve the work so they can meet their intended goal.

The goal might be to attract the attention of an agent or publisher. Or it might be to ensure that the self-publishing writer looks absolutely brilliant when the book representing their work or philosophy soars into the hands of the buying public.

If you're a first-time author, and you are unfamiliar with the editing process, it's a good idea to educate yourself about what's available out there, and then decide what type of editor is most appropriate for your work.

The editing function generally divvies up into three main categories: content editing, copy editing and proof-reading.

Content editing is the first pass an editor might make through your book to see how it's put together and whether or not it's logically organized. Content editing might also be called developmental, substantive, or structural editing. It will usually include:

• Revising or moving entire paragraphs or sentences

• Adding new material to fill in gaps

• Deleting original material that doesn't work

• Re-organizing and restructuring content to improve flow and clarity

An editor might or might not correct language issues at this point, but if there are paragraphs where the meaning is unclear they will flag them for clarification: if the reader doesn't understand what's being said, it's impossible to know whether the content is in the right place.

Copy editing involves a detailed look at each paragraph, sentence and word in the manuscript to ensure consistency and clarity. This type of editing is also called line, mechanical, or stylistic editing. It's very detailed and focused on precision. Copy editing involves:

• Ensuring consistency of character, story and setting

• Ensuring that the details included contribute to the story overall, rather than distract from it

• Ensuring that the story is largely "shown, not told"

You need an editor with a good eye for detail here, as well as someone who can easily see the "Big Picture" of what's going on in the story.

Proofreading is the final step towards completion of a manuscript and it involves a very basic check for errors around such issues as:

• Spelling

• Grammar (contractions, verb-noun agreement)

• Punctuation and

• Word choice

Not all editors provide all types of editing. I can work at all three levels but I ask clients to tell me ahead of time how much involvement they want me to have in their manuscript – the more input I provide, the longer it takes to come up with a finished product, and that raises the job's ultimate cost.

Generally, however, clients will ask me to jump in and work my magic on all levels, which means I take a couple of passes through the manuscript. I have a long and varied career in writing behind me, and one that's been augmented by a ton of training in all sorts of interesting areas, so I bring a lot to the "editing table."

 The issues I generally need to focus on most in manuscripts include:

•   Grammar and general English usage

•   Flow – i.e. the flow of language from one sentence to the next, one paragraph to the next and one chapter to the next

•   Order and overall structure

•   Information omissions – i.e. has anything been left out of the story that maybe should be there?

•   Work around presuppositions – we often assume that what we know is what everyone else knows and we get so close to our work that we sometimes don't catch ourselves at that particular game. I can identify presuppositions and correct for audience awareness so an author is truly talking a language his or her audience will understand.

•   Thematic unity – personally I work thematically with every document I write as I find it is a powerful way to engage audience attention. I can work a theme into a text as a touchstone to help carry readers from start to finish in a consistent and satisfying manner

• Metaphors – these are powerful ways of engaging audience support for a story and I work them smoothly into a manuscript where appropriate

• Audience inclusion – I am trained in many techniques for writing to develop audience rapport and I incorporate these techniques into a text

• Story telling – stories are the most powerful way to teach and I can embellish or refine a story to make it as inspirational as the occasion demands

• Subtle promotion (non-fiction business books) – does the client need to be positioned as an expert authority on a topic at key points in the document?

• Keyword inclusion if requested.

It takes a great deal of effort to write a book and I am very respectful of the heart and energy my clients have invested in their manuscripts. Ask a prospective editor what type of editing they are able to provide and what type of editing they like doing best. The skill set required to do a "big picture" analysis of what's out of place in the overall storyline is different from the skill set required to catch tiny grammatical details; few people can do both well and it's best to know first if your editor can provide this capability so you won't be disappointed.

Question #3 What About Your Voice?

Most authors are very protective of their Voice and there's a fine line between "fixing" a text into technical perfection and utterly destroying the mood and intention the writer had in mind. (Believe me, I've been edited too and I know how awful that can feel!)

Some writers are also wary of having their writing "*judged*" by someone else and they fear that the tampering an editor can inflict on a work of literature could potentially destroy it.

These are very good concerns and I know from experience that some editors are a little ham-fisted with the red pencil. In addition, not all editors are writers and some might not understand the complex emotional fabric of a story.

Technical excellence does not always come packaged with sensitivity or visionary thinking. Again, asking a few questions before you start will arm you with a set of expectations that will serve you well.

It's safe to say that undergoing the editorial process can be a nerve-wracking experience for some people, especially those who have not spent their careers in fields where editing is a standard part of the information-output process.

People may also feel a little vulnerable if their school experiences have trained them to believe that they are not good writers. If that's the case, hiring an editor can feel like inviting more judgement.

It doesn't need to!

If you are already a writer, or are thought of as a darned good one, you might have the added concern of wondering if hiring an editor might detract from your reputation, and that can be a stressful thought as well.

I myself hired an editor to review my novel manuscript and it was money well worth spending. I didn't have to accept all the changes my editor suggested (and I didn't!) But she did provide another set of eyes to eliminate hyperbole and question character motivation at times.

As an editor myself, I like to take the potential sting out of the editing process by telling people that we are each on our own writing continuum and there is always more opportunity to improve. I started writing professionally in 1982 and have had incredible training in many writing fields. And although I am a published author and a successful businessperson, I am *still* looking for opportunities to improve. My clients may not have been focusing their efforts so diligently on becoming great writers but they HAVE been investing themselves in other experiences that are equally valuable.

When editing, I focus on ensuring that the magnificent ideas my clients have come up with are translated into language that their audience can instantly recognize as compelling and important...while still ensuring the words reflect the author's very own voice.

The goal of hiring an editor should be to make the work as powerful as possible, in whatever way the author feels that should be, while ensuring that the author's voice is protected and, at times, enhanced.

The errors do need to be fixed, in order to ensure the work's credibility. But this can be done carefully and respectfully. When it comes right down to it, this is really an issue of trust: before hiring an editor, make sure you feel confident that feel they will protect your Voice.

Question #4 How much does editing cost?

I find it very difficult to provide a ballpark figure for how much editing a manuscript might cost. The final cost depends on the length of the manuscript, the level of my involvement and the language skill of the originating author. I tend to suggest clients decide how much of my "me-ness" they want me to provide and start me off with a five-page sample.

From there I can identify what the primary challenges are going to be and provide an estimate for editing the entire manuscript, along with an assessment of overall writing strengths *and* opportunities for improvement. I do charge for this service and if you're interested please get in touch.

If cost is an issue, I am also open to the idea of providing an initial edit of the first three chapters and then leaving my client to review the rest of the manuscript with my comments and suggestions in mind. Once they've taken another pass at the manuscript, I can recommence.

This is all fun work for me and it allows me to draw on a wealth of professional writing experiences. I have an MA in English Language and Writing and I speak five languages (three well). I'm also certified as a General and a Master Practitioner of Neurolinguistic Programming. All of these accomplishments have been a huge benefit to my understanding of audience, motivation and language patterns.

Part of what my clients get with me is a voice of support. Bringing a book to life can be a lonely experience at the same time as it is an overwhelming and exciting one. Having done it myself, I understand how much perseverance it takes.

That said, the editing of a manuscript is an investment that can easily run into thousands of dollars. Different editors charge different rates, depending on their skill, training and experience. Some charge by the word, others by the hour. As in just about any field, the higher the fee, the more expertise you can generally expect to be applied to your manuscript.

Question #5 What about Your Vision?

Most people begin writing a book in response to a spark of imaginative delight that makes them feel they have something important they want to share with the world.

Some folks can't help it. They just "need" to get the story out onto paper. Other people have more practical reasons for writing: as businesspeople (often with a speaking career on the go), they have a philosophy or system that they would like to explain through the exciting medium of a published book. They want to change how things are done in the world or support their reputation in some manner.

I define these motivations as "visionary." A book almost always starts with a dream and it is the dream of being a published author that has kick-started many a literary career. But when we get right down to it, the process of writing itself is not always visionary.

Non-fiction writers need an overall plan for their book and a well-defined sense of what each chapter will contain.

The unrolling of a business book is often similar to a university paper, with an introduction, a list of the main points, a list of all the sub-points, a few examples, and a conclusion. This is a very linear process.

The unfolding of a creative work might be a little messier but the author still needs a storyline, outlines for each characters, some progression through character development and a great concluding chapter that rewards the reader for reading through to the end. This is also a substantially linear process.

And, from a reader's perspective, a written work must make sense — that means that the linear aspect of a written work is key. But I contend that a written work also has to speak to people's hearts as well.

The best non-fiction books don't just fill our heads with sobering and fascinating intellectual information. They also move us to a higher level of emotional understanding as well.

And it should go without saying that a great novel is an emotional journey that connects us more securely with how we think *and* feel.

When selecting an editor it's a good idea to ensure that the individual you are going to work with understands not just the linear delight of the reading equation, but also the emotional mathematics as well. You, as the author, deserve to be respected for the dream quest you are on to bring your book to life.

And your readers will be best served if you can connect with them, at some level, in an emotional manner as well. You don't want to knock people over with sappy prose. You just want to acknowledge that we are all on a journey that inevitably engages our hearts. When people finish reading your book, you may want them to *know* something. But it's more powerful when your readers *feel* something as well.

A great editor will be able to seamlessly insert that emotional content into your manuscript. And, at the same time, they will support you most if they can help support the vision that you, as the author, have for the book you are bringing to life.

A few final words

If you'd like to continue the conversation we've started here on writing with strength and elegance, I can offer a few different ideas. You can:

1. **Hire me to speak to your group or organization on any topic of writing that is relevant to you.** I have 30 years of writing experience upon which to draw, and I am a published author with two books to my credit. Speaking (and listening!) are fun for me and I'd be more than happy to put my skills at your disposal.

2. **Hire me to coach you in your own writing evolution.** I take on a limited number of coaching clients for whom I develop customized training programs designed to help them hit the next level in their development. I also provide coaching to help you move beyond a period of being "stuck in the mud" of life, as well as coaching around the achievement of specific goals.

3. **Hire me to edit your work.** I am a sensitive but vigilant editor (fiction and non-fiction genres) and writer and you can hire me to take a look at your existing document or manuscript and revise it to a new level of excellence. I can be reached at: susan@crossmancommunications.com or +1-905-469-1892 or on Skype at SusanCrossman (Canada)

Chapter 4: The Benefits of Coaching

Prelude:

From Passages to Epiphany by Susan Crossman – An Introduction

A big fat grey squirrel balanced himself on the snow bank just outside my kitchen window and twitched his bushy tail. My little friend was clutching a nut in his paws with great authority and he was gnawing at it with energy and skill. Little flecks of brown scattered onto the snow at his feet as he prised the meat from its shell. The sun shone high in a brilliant blue sky that day, and its rays glanced off the snow and splintered into a billion glittering crystals. I stared intently at the scene beyond the borders of my house and I drank in the beauty, the peace and the radiance of what had been put before me. I felt full of gratitude for that precious morsel of visual delight and I promised myself I would return to the memory of that sweet little squirrel later in the day, as often as possible in fact, as a reminder that good things can still exist in the middle of trauma.

This was a moment of awakening for me, a moment where it felt like a veil had been lifted from my understanding to usher me into a larger awareness of the world around me. I could see there was much more available to me in life than the burdens that were engulfing me at the time and although I was choking back tears, my load was significantly lightened by the small gift of peace the squirrel had given me.

I held my breath and marvelled at the many different colours in that little squirrel's fur, at his perfectly matched eyes and the audacious fluffiness of his beautiful fat tail. I could see the delicate detail of his claws as he wrapped them firmly around his treasure. I felt connected to his world in a novel and touching way. I had never looked at an animal so intently before. The sight of him took my breath away.

After a few minutes, the squirrel bounded gracefully away, perhaps to find another nut, or play on the fence that ran around the perimeter of our backyard. I returned to rinsing the hypodermic syringe that I had just used to inject my dying husband's arm with morphine, and I took three deep breaths. There was still much to endure that endless day, and now I had been given a gift that would help ferry me through it. I've had many moments I would call "awakenings" prior to and since that painful passage some years ago. My beloved husband did ultimately pass away, as we all must in turn, and my children and I journeyed on into new lives filled with both challenges and opportunities. I haven't always seen the bright side of the road, let alone walked on it. And I haven't always felt blessed by a soaring spirit. But I have been consistently aware of those moments when a little part of me said "Aha!" as some new knowledge, insight or understanding floated into my orbit.

Excerpt from "Passages to Epiphany" By Susan Crossman Manor House Publishing, 2012

When I wrote the preceding words for my book, "Passages to Epiphany," I wasn't specifically talking about coaching but I almost could have been: good coaching inevitably involves a process of awakening. A coach serves as a guide, a mentor, and a poser of questions we never thought to ask of ourselves. Or perhaps never wanted to. They nudge us *towards* a greater connection to ourselves and help us see the world from a new perspective. They can help us move towards the things we want in life and *away from* the things we don't want.

While I find that coaching people can be a marvellously creative experience, and a very exciting one, it also benefits from a specific process and a structure.

I became a coach after years of studying how values, behaviour and beliefs affect motivation and performance. As a writer, I needed to understand these issues well so I could write compelling marketing and PR copy for my clients, and create engaging characters for my fiction writing.

At the same time, I myself was engaging coaches to fuel my own growth and development. There came a moment in time and space when I put the two ideas together and realized I wanted to help other people move beyond their own "blockages" so life could flow more smoothly for them.

I now provide two types of coaching: Goal Coaching to help people meet specific goals and ``Calm the Chaos`` coaching to help people stop feeling stuck and start connecting to what is in their highest and best interest in life.

I initially didn't understand what a coach was, or whether hiring one represented the right road for me. I'm an independent person and I don't like the idea of someone telling me what to do. But I eventually realized that if I wanted to grow – and if I wanted my business to grow – I was going to have to see my world through someone else's eyes. That person would have to be someone who could give me ideas I hadn't thought of before and suggestions for generating the results I sought. They would have to be able to wake me up to possibilities I had not previously considered.

If you are at the same fork in the road, I invite you to ask a few questions to help you clarify what you need next. And I would start with:

1. Do you need a coach?

I'll be honest: I think we can all benefit from coaching. I hired my first coach when I realized that I had goals and dreams and no real concept of how to move towards them. And while I'm a well-educated person and very, very sensible, I realized that I was also hampered to some extent by the paradigms I had created for myself. I needed someone who could objectively look at my beliefs and behaviours and help me figure out where I was blocking myself from greater results.

You might need a coach if:

• You aren't moving towards your goals and dreams as quickly as you'd like

• You feel there's something missing in your approach to what you're doing but you aren't quite sure what it is or

• You need a high-level "accountability partner" to hold you to your program for success

Coaching is not counselling or therapy. If you have serious issues that need to be addressed, then you are better served by a qualified counsellor or therapist.

What type of coach is best?

There are countless coaches available in this world, and many of them are excellent people with superb coaching skills. But fit is important.

I once spent 18 months looking for the right business coach and it was time well spent. I interviewed prospective coaches to learn why they had decided to become a coach, what their areas of specialty were, how they worked and what kind of results they typically helped clients achieve. I was thrilled with the person I ultimately selected.

The best way to find the best person for your particular needs is to talk to people. Find out who your friends, acquaintances and colleagues are coaching with and talk to them about their coaching experiences. Then go and talk to their coaches to see whether you connect well with them.

If you don't feel that little "click" inside that tells you there's a good fit, then move on. Coaching can involve a big investment of time and money and you need to have a high level of trust in the person you are hiring to guide you.

I suggest you also ask yourself if you feel better and brighter after talking to a prospective coach or drained and depleted. A good coach is a person who will bring positive energy to your world and you shouldn't have to settle for anything less.

2. How Does Coaching Work?

Every coach works a little differently, but in general your coaching package will include a set number of conversations with your coach wherein you will discuss your current challenges and develop a plan of action around them.

You may be assigned some "homework" at the end of each session that has been designed to help you move towards your goal and break through any challenges you've been having.

Ideally, a coaching session will generate a number of "Aha!" moments for you where you suddenly get an understanding you didn't have previously.

These new insights are yours forever! And they allow you to take a fresh look at what you're doing and how you're doing it with new choices in your beliefs and in your behaviour. It can be quite magical!

3. What are the Benefits of Coaching?

My own coaches have helped me experience extraordinary growth on personal, financial and spiritual levels. Having people I trust bring their insights and understanding, wisdom and integrity to the issues I've had to tussle with has helped me tune my performance ever higher so I can fill my life and business with the success I desire.

A successful coaching experience might help you:

• Gain clarity on issues that have been creating anxiety for you

• Set goals for future successes

• Map out a plan of action for getting where you want to go

• Eliminate limiting beliefs that may have been holding you back

• Develop greater confidence in your own skills and abilities

• Introduce you to new strategies and tactics for generating success

• Identify habits and behaviours that have not been supporting your success

• Stay focused on what you want in life

• Learn to celebrate your achievements

It's extremely rewarding to feel the delight of understanding dawning within when you finally become aware of what's been holding you back; it's even more delightful to start moving forward again.

If you would like to know more about how I might be able to coach you towards the successes you would like to experience, please contact me at 905-469-1892 or at susan@crossmancommunications.com.

I was in enough to get along with people. I was never socially inarticulate. Not a loner. And that saved my life, saved my sanity. That and the writing. But to this day I distrust anybody who thought school was a good time.
— **Stephen King**

Reduce your plan to writing. The moment you complete this, you will have definitely given concrete form to the intangible desire.
— **Napoleon Hill**

You have to write the book that wants to be written. And if the book will be too difficult for grown-ups, then you write it for children.
— **Madeleine L'Engle**

What really knocks me out is a book that, when you're all done reading it, you wish the author that wrote it was a terrific friend of yours and you could call him up on the phone whenever you felt like it.
— **J.D. Salinger**

Substitute 'damn' every time you're inclined to write 'very;' your editor will delete it and the writing will be just as it should be.
— **Mark Twain**

Geniuses can be scintillating and geniuses can be somber, but it's that inescapable sorrowful depth that shines through — originality.
— **Jack Kerouac**

Chapter 5: Business Writing Tips

As a writer and editor I see written material at all levels of competency and as I like to tell the clients who seek my editorial input on their book-writing projects, we are each on our own writing continuum. I believe it's always possible to improve, and that continued practice and learning is the key to development.

I've provided material for the corporate communications departments of a number of multi-national organizations and have often been impressed by the level of professionalism and capability of employees in these areas of a company; at the same time, I've also heard executives in other departments bemoan the language skills of employees whose main purpose is to do something other than write.

Writing is a key skill that relates directly to a company's bottom line and the higher the level of literacy in an organization, the more likely that company will be to meet goals, enhance relationships and generate revenue. Strong communication creates results, and that is true in every form of business correspondence, from simple emails to annual reports. There's no wiggling out of it: a business needs employees who can communicate fluidly and effectively.

I had the great good fortune to be in the audience when former CEO of Franklin-Covey—and fervent champion of the English language—Hyrum Smith spoke recently. He noted that there are approximately 343,000 words in the English language and he told listeners that Winston Churchill had the highest working vocabulary of any human being ever known at about 25,000 words.

The average business person, by contrast, has a working vocabulary of 12,000 words. And the average teenager in North America right now has a working vocabulary of 2,300 words.

Shocking, isn't it?

What is the future of our country and our economy if we are not grooming young people to speak and write clearly, comprehensively and persuasively?

While format changes from one type of business document to another, if your job requires you to demonstrate any degree of language facility at all, you might want to keep these ideas in mind when you're developing your next document:

Skip the buzz words

Every industry sector, and probably every company, comes complete with a standard range of terms and phrases that slip off the tongues of people in every department and end up mangling a perfectly good language. For example:

Decisioning. Ugh! A team doesn't meet so they can get busy decisioning. They might make decisions or deliberate, or problem-solve. But they do not decision;

Learnings, as in "There were many learnings in the experience." The proper term is "lessons" or, in a pinch, "takeaways;"

Solutionize, as in, "Together as a team we can solutionize the situation." Pretty please, throw that word out and use the correct one, which is "solve;"

Wordsmith, used as a verb, as in "Melva can go and wordsmith the document and then we'll send it upstairs." I practically stamp my feet in frustration when I hear that one. Melva might well be a wonderful wordsmith but she will be editing that document, not wordsmithing it.

You get the drift. Make it a habit to sniff out unconventional uses of your language and critically ask yourself if they are contributing to a better understanding of your idea, or fogging up the landscape. I'm all for creativity. But not at the expense of meaning.

Watch out for Redundancies

We tend to default to common usage in a lot of our writing and unfortunately common usage is sometimes sloppy. I hate to be a tyrant about language but there's no advantage to using more words than necessary to get your point across. They take up more space and occupy more of people's valuable time, so precision is everyone's friend. Here are a handful of offenders that you might want to eliminate from your writing playbook:

Absolutely certain. Certain already means without doubt. Absolutely doesn't add any value.

Added bonus. A bonus is already something extra so the word "added" isn't necessary.

Advance warning. A warning is already something that happens ahead of an event; the word "advance" doesn't make it happen any earlier.

Ask a question. What else can one ask? An answer? You can't ask something without involving a question so the word "question" is redundant.

Basic essentials. Essentials are as basic as you can get already; you don't need the adjective!

Came at a time when. *When* provides the necessary temporal reference to the action of coming; "at a time" is redundant.

Close proximity. Proximity already means close so pick one or the other.

Difficult dilemma. A dilemma is by definition something difficult to resolve so the word "difficult" is unnecessary.

Direct confrontation. A confrontation involves head-to-head conflict and it doesn't get any more direct than that!

End result. A result is already at the end of a process; omit the word "end."

Estimated at roughly. The word "estimate" already tells the reader that the quantity is an approximation; the word "roughly" (or, often, "about") is unnecessary.

Final outcome. An outcome can't help being final!

First began. A beginning is whatever happened first so that word is unnecessary.

Foreign imports. Imports by their very nature are foreign. Lose the word "foreign."

Free gift. Aren't gifts always free?

Major breakthrough. Isn't a breakthrough intrinsically major? A breakthrough is a significant progress in an effort and the notable nature of the event is implicit.

Past history. History is what happened in the past so ditch the "past!"

Plan ahead. Since planning is what occurs ahead of time anyway we don't need to add in the word "ahead."

Protest against. A protest implies opposition so the word "against" is unnecessary.

Repeat again. To repeat already means to say something again so the word "again" is redundant.

Revert back. Well, we can't exactly revert forward, can we? Ditch the "word back!"

Sudden explosion. If an event occurs gradually it cannot be an explosion; omit the word "sudden."

Unexpected surprise. If a surprise is expected it is not a surprise! Delete "unexpected."

Written down. The word "down" is redundant.

Use Detail and Think Big

We know from studies in learning and psychology that some people are adept at big picture thinking and others are absolute maniacs with detail. Great writing incorporates both, but one of the biggest challenges I've seen among my editing clients is the tendency to default to the conceptual at the expense of the detail. I want to know that a new project will revolutionize product sales at my company, of course. But tell me why, tell me how and tell me what the end results are going to be!

Show, Rather than Tell

This is a key concept for success in the creative writing stratosphere and it's no less important in the business world. You can tell people how great your program is until you run out of oxygen and they'll actually believe it when you provide them with proof. Judicious use of statistics, graphs and images, as well as actual case study story-telling, is far more compelling than a mere statement of unproven "fact."

Avoid Common Errors

There are a lot of wrong turns you can take in English and a slight deviation from standard practice can affect your credibility and muddle your meaning. I see a lot of errors in the use of tenses in my work so it's a good idea to invest in some good grammar training if you feel this is not an area of strength for you. This book is not intended to be a grammar training manual — plenty of other people have tackled that far more effectively than I ever could. But the following list may help you avoid some common faux-pas I see:

Apostrophes. We only use them to denote the fact that one or more letters are missing (won't , don't, can't, shouldn't, etc.) or to show possession. (Janet's report, Henry's computer).

Bated breath. Not "baited breath!"

Could of, would of and should of. They are all incorrect! The proper wording is could have, would have and should have.

Edition vs. addition. Edition is about a publication (e.g. the 12th edition of the book, the fourth edition of a magazine). Addition is about adding numbers together.

E.g. vs. i.e. E.g. is the abbreviation of the Latin words, "exempli gratia" (meaning "for example"). We use it this way: "I appreciate the classical musicians, e.g. Bach, Mozart and Handel." I.e. is the abbreviation of the Latin "id est," meaning "that is to say." I would use it this way: "Of all the music available today, I like Bach, Mozart and Handel the best, i.e. I prefer classical music."

Into vs. in to. We can walk into a room or go into a business but we go in to see the dentist.

It's vs. its. It's a contraction of the words "it is." (It's raining out!) Its denotes possession (The dog lifted its paw.)

Me vs. I. "I" functions as the subject of a sentence, the person doing the action. "John and I are going skiing." "Me" is always used with a preposition. "John is coming with me."

Peak, peek and pique. A mountain has a peak, a quick look is a peek and when I'm curious it means something has piqued my curiosity.

Then vs. than. "Then" is about time ("I read the news and then I checked the weather."). "Than" is used to make a comparison ("I was less energetic today than you were!")

Ultimate vs. Penultimate. Ultimate is the very last one; penultimate is the second last one. "November is the penultimate month in the year."

A 360 Degree Turn. This implies you are back where you started. A 180 degree turn, by contrast, means you completely reversed direction.

There are plenty more and I suggest that if you're interested you might want to do an online search to learn more of the most common mistakes people make with their writing.

Proofread Everything!

I know how easy it is to skip this crucial step in the writing process – we're all busy and many people barely have enough time to develop a rough draft of the project they've been assigned, let alone polish it into practical perfection. That's a formula for linguistic suicide. The more clear you can be in your communication, the more likely you are to generate the results you seek. Here are a few ideas to make the proofing phase more palatable:

Start with a "big picture" scan of what you've written. Have you included all the major ideas? Have you left anything out? Do you need to delete any irrelevant information? Is everything in the right place?

Go through your document and delete any unnecessary words. I've written a lot of newsletter material over the years and sometimes space requirements change partway through a project and I need to cut a 500-word article down to 200. I start by seeing how far I can get by simply tightening up every sentence and trying to replace five words with two or three. It's surprising how easy this is and it often shows me where I've been too wordy (lazy?) in the first place.

Read the document aloud to catch any spelling mistakes or grammatical errors – often your ear will pick them up more readily than your eyes will.

Take breaks. Sometimes we get so close to our work that we miss glaring errors or omissions. Often a walk around the block can make a world of difference to our ability to read critically. A break of an entire day or three is beneficial as well, so if you can afford the time off, always take it.

Print the document and read it on paper. Studies have shown that the human eye is not always perfectly suited to screen reading, whereas reading printed letters on actual paper is a much easier and accurate way to process information.

Use your computer's Spell-check. Critically. Spell-check is sometimes wrong and the more you learn about the English language, the more confident you can be in deciding whether or not to accept the changes Spellcheck recommends.

Those who find ugly meanings in beautiful things are corrupt without being charming. This is a fault. Those who find beautiful meanings in beautiful things are the cultivated. For these there is hope. They are the elect to whom beautiful things mean only Beauty. There is no such thing as a moral or an immoral book. Books are well written, or badly written. That is all.
— **Oscar Wilde**

Read, read, read. Read everything -- trash, classics, good and bad, and see how they do it. Just like a carpenter who works as an apprentice and studies the master. Read! You'll absorb it. Then write. If it's good, you'll find out. If it's not, throw it out of the window.
— **William Faulkner**

The most important things are the hardest to say. They are the things you get ashamed of, because words diminish them – words shrink things that seemed limitless when they were in your head to no more than living size when they're brought out. But it's more than that, isn't it? The most important things lie too close to wherever your secret heart is buried, like landmarks to a treasure your enemies would love to steal away. And you may make revelations that cost you dearly only to have people look at you in a funny way, not understanding what you've said at all, or why you thought it was so important that you almost cried while you were saying it. That's the worst, I think. When the secret stays locked within not for want of a teller but for want of an understanding ear.
— **Stephen King**

Chapter 6: Beating Writer's Block

What About Writer's Block?

Is there any writing term more famous than "Writer's Block?" It's almost a legendary concept and even after decades of professional writing experience I still have those occasional moments when the words just won't come. They park themselves stubbornly beyond the veil of my accessible reality, nonchalantly filing their nails or humming cheerfully to themselves while I drive myself into an increasing frenzy of frustration.

It becomes something of a game between us: I go grab another cup of coffee. The words stay away. I make a couple of phone calls. The words stay away. I tidy my desk....

If I'm working on a piece of non-fiction or a business-related document the problem can sometimes be traced to insufficient information. I tend to over-research almost everything I write so that I can pick and choose from only the very best factual information. So sometimes when Writer's Block hits, I immediately check to see if I need to do a little more research.

At other times, my head is so cluttered with other things that are going on in my life that I simply can't settle down to work.

There I sit, hunched over my keyboard hoping to write, when suddenly my mind is ping-ponging at Olympic speed between intruding thoughts: another project, the dog's epilepsy, my recent tax statement, the rabbit's litter training, hopes for an upcoming holiday, the meat I forgot to take out of the freezer for dinner … and who knows what else?

If that happens to you, be kind to yourself. Step. Away. From. The. Desk. Go for a walk. Clear your head. Ponder. Collect those errant thoughts and words in a nice wicker basket in your head and think about what you want to write about as though it were a cherished friend.

Allow ideas and phrases to take over your mind and enjoy the fresh air (or, if you are in a city, the gentle smog). Let the piece start writing itself in your head. After a decent period of time, say at least half an hour, revisit your computer and start to type. Expand on what you wrote in your head.

It's a good idea to keep a notebook with you at all times so you can jot down words and phrases, thoughts and ideas, as they pop into your head at odd times of the day – while you're sitting on a bus, for example, or standing in the grocery line. Capturing them for later use is actually also a time-saving device as well, since you will gradually build up a library of brilliant expressions that are available to you anytime, anywhere.

Some people like to take a break from their writing before they finish a thought so they can get right back to work as soon as they return. It's like a kindly kick-start to your writing flow and, of course, once you are in the flow of writing you are usually able to keep going.

These tips might also be helpful:

- Schedule your writing time well

- Stay away from online distractions

- Give yourself a deadline

But this all brings me to another topic, which is the process of writing itself. I've been asked before what the "right" way to do it is and I'm afraid that's a judgement I cannot make. While I've made some suggestions that work for me and the people I coach in the section on structuring your writing, it really shouldn't matter to anyone else whether you're sitting with your laptop on the living room floor or on a cozy chair in your back garden. The "right" way for you is the one that brings you the best results.

The key issue here is finding what brings you the best results and for that you might need to play with your time and your location. Personally I need a room where there are no distractions, and that often means getting out of my office where the phone might ring, other projects might call and just a glance around the room might remind me that I need to order another printer cartridge or fill my water jug. There is a quiet room at my local library where conversation is not allowed and I often lug my laptop over there, plug in my headphones (I listen to Chamber music) and get right down to work.

I also need a long interrupted period of time in order to write smoothly. Trying to fit any half-way decent writing into a spare half hour between meetings does not work for me at all. But three hours on a Tuesday afternoon does. In fact, I try to keep my weekday afternoons free in order to have those large blocks of time available to write, and that seems to work well for me.

Finally, I need to be rested. If I am over-tired I don't write (or edit) well. Ever. The words swim in front of my eyes and I am capable of reading the same sentence seven or eight times with nary a critical thought in mind. I'm up by 5:00 a.m. every weekday morning and I often don't get to bed before 11:00 at night. My days are packed with all the hectic racing that a modern life demands. I do get tired! But because people pay me to write and edit, there is an integrity issue involved for me: they are not paying for my worst efforts, they are paying for my best. When I'm tired I conscientiously do the only thing I possibly can do to rectify the matter: I take a nap.

Half an hour of guilt-free sleep is usually all it takes to bring my energy back up again and I can resume my writing or editing with renewed efficiency and focus.

Writing is a magical occupation and doing it well is gratifying. But feel free to develop your own way of going about it – what works for me might not necessarily work for you and the point isn't to match someone else's idea of "Right," but rather to get the job done as effectively and gracefully as possible.

Chapter 7: Cashing in on Content

We've all heard the old chestnut that says that the only constant in our world is change itself, and I've found over the 30-plus years of my career that this is particularly true of business and marketing writing. I'm old enough to have been writing when the internet first poked its opportunity onto my desktop computer and, in fact, I'm old enough to remember typing articles out on a manual typewriter.

Resistance was futile in each of those cases and had I decided to ignore the technological advances that merely heralded the arrival of the next ones, I would not have been able to maintain a career as a writer. So if I can give any advice to anyone who wants or needs to get their message across to an important audience it is this: keep learning!

Furthermore, I believe that the revolution has only just begun and that we will continue to see an evolution in marketing and revenue generation as long as there is electricity to power our mobile devices. Pretending they aren't happening won't make them go away. And while there still seems to be a place for direct mail and there is definitely a role for networking in the development of our businesses, I believe that developing and polishing our online content is the key to the kingdom.

I take a CASH-related approach to content development. In order to see success in online marketing we need:

Clarity – around the messages we want our perfect audience to receive about our product or service, as well as clarity around a content marketing strategy that is specifically geared to our target audience.

Action – so we take the steps necessary to appeal to our perfect clients

Success Strategies– which are about confidently executing our content marketing strategy and

Habits – that support a continued online content program.

I get really excited about content marketing because it's an inexpensive way to differentiate ourselves in the marketplace while helping our perfect clients get to know, like and trust our businesses and the people who run them. Most business people like to make money.

Most of us would also like to make more. Let's face it, the effort required to build and run a successful business is huge. It takes a great deal of dedication, as well as countless hours and unlimited energy. If we can find a way to streamline the process so that we can reach more people with less effort — and a moderate investment — wouldn't we want to do that? Of course we would. That's where your online content marketing strategy comes in.

A Content Marketing Strategy is part of your marketing strategy, part of your Search Engine Optimization strategy, a way to keep your business name favourably in front of your target audience, a way to educate prospective clients and a way to motivate prospective clients.

I'm passionate about content marketing for a number of reasons. First of all, I think the huge shakeout in the economy over the past half-dozen years has meant that we are now moving towards a world where almost all business is done online and if you aren't playing in that field you aren't going to have a business.

Secondly, it's really been working for me and I am on a rampage of sharing these days to help other businesses get up and running so they can make the money they desire and be the difference they want to be in the world.

I know a lot of business owners who feel they should learn more about social media and content marketing but have been pretty much stalled at the station because they didn't have a clue how to go about doing it, or it seemed dumb, or it felt like one more thing they had to add to an already overloaded task list.

If you fall into that category, may I respectfully suggest you get over that obstacle so you can tame the content monster and make some money with your message? You deserve to be successful!

It can be done!

Let me tell you a bit about my story. As many people know, I'm a career writer who started writing professionally in 1982, and in fact I have only ever worked with words. I've had stints as a journalist, a government communicator, a marketing copywriter and a corporate communicator. I'm also the author of three traditionally published books. The first one, called "Shades of Teale," is a novel about a woman's experience of an abusive marriage. My second book, entitled, "Passages to Epiphany," is a collection of short stories and creative-non-fiction pieces about awakenings. And the book you are currently reading contains some of the writing wisdom I've collected up over the years that I think is imperative for other people – writers and non-writers alike — to know.

I have what I would describe as a magical life that allows me to balance career and motherhood, contribution and enjoyment.

Five years ago I was minding my own business, playing with my writing, working on my novel, hanging out with my husband and planning both a trip to Barbados and the purchase of a lakeside cottage in Vermont.

I lived in a very large house in Beaconsfield, Quebec, and life was pretty idyllic. So you can imagine what a shock it was when my 49-year-old husband was diagnosed with terminal stomach cancer.

He was painfully ill for three months and then he died. Steve had been my high school sweetheart and together we had two young kids, at that time aged seven and nine years old. Our blended family also included my daughter from my first marriage and my two step-kids. It was a traumatic time for all of us and I was in shock at how quickly life can change. It was a miserable lesson.

Not only had I lost my best friend, but I realized I had to kiss good-bye all my fancy dreams of the future, get out of my 4,500 square foot house, and figure out how I was going to raise my kids and create enough income that I could financially support my disabled mother, should the time come when that might be necessary.

In the mirage of delight that came with being married to a man who at the time of his death was a successful currency trader, I had not worked too hard in a few years. My business had become a pleasant hobby. It wasn't making anywhere near enough money to support me, my kids and my mother.

I decided to move back to my home province of Ontario with my children and I dug in for a year or two of complete trauma and emotional chaos. When the dust settled, I realized a lot had been happening in the business world while I had been more or less playing at being a writer.

I was hearing strange words like "social media marketing" and "search engine optimization." This "content" word was being bandied about. And I realized I didn't have a clue how to run a writing business in the internet world.

So I rolled up my sleeves and learned everything I could possibly learn about how people were communicating and marketing themselves online.

I'm sure you can imagine how challenging that was.

There will probably be a few readers of this book who find themselves equally panicked and I invite you to reach out to me either for help with your online content or for coaching to help you make sense of a painful experience. Aside from being a writer who specializes in online content, I am a certified Awakening Coach and it's a process that has helped me come to the place of contentment that I currently enjoy. I love sharing the abundance-oriented experience with others.

Concept 1:   Clarity Around Concept Marketing

Did you know that some sources currently estimate that 80% of all business is being done online now?

And according to the Roper Public Affairs company, 80% of business decision makers prefer to get company information in a series of articles versus an advertisement.

70% of the Roper survey's respondents said that content marketing makes them feel closer to the sponsoring company, while 60% say that company content helps them make better product decisions.

So what would it be like if your customer looked forward to receiving your marketing? What if, when they received it, they spent 15, 30, even 45 minutes with it?

And what if they learned to know, like and trust you so much through your online content that they became and stayed loyal customers?

Doesn't it make sense that you'd better have a very strong presence online if you want to be competitive?

I like to use the story of Red Bull's marketing as an illustration: Red Bull is an energy drink company that runs something called the Red Bull Content Pool. It stocks more than 50,000 photos and 5,000 videos about sports, culture and lifestyle. They make the material available to their 4.8-

million subscribers, which tend to be TV stations, platform providers and cinema distributors.

Why do they do that? Does the content they provide talk about how amazing the Red Bull drink is? NO! But it says reams about Red Bull as a lifestyle.

Red Bull's strategy is all about aligning the company's image with its target market's sense of who they are as well. When those two match, you have the beginnings of customer loyalty.

Content marketing is all about informing people without working too hard at selling them. The theory is that if you provide lots of valuable information you will show people that you are an expert in your field and lead them to a state where they know, like and trust you so much that they simply want to do business with you.

The more ways you can find to do this, the bigger profile you develop, and the more you shine. If you do this well, you will make it obvious to anyone looking for the service you provide that you are the ONLY choice in the field, and your competition will fade into the background by comparison.

Last year, I was able to trace 44 per cent of my business revenue directly or indirectly to the content I had placed online about me and my business. Because I'm a writer, my outlay for my online content was limited to the time I spent, but other businesses may want to hire a writer to do it for them. Either way, it's substantially less expensive than buying paid advertising space in either a print or online publication.

I don't believe that content marketing can totally replace personal networking. You still want face-to-face opportunities to meet people and develop ways for them to get to know you and your business. But your online content management strategy is a great way to support any other marketing you do. People might meet you at a networking event but if they are remotely interested in doing business with you they are going to search you out online.

So first of all, you want to have material available that routes people directly to you and, secondly, you want the material people find online about you to be consistent with your brand.

Just for fun, I invite you to do an online search of you or your business. What do you find?

Next, search out a competitor.

Are there more references to them online than there are about you? Are they on quality websites? Do they have a lot of links to their website? If you don't compare favourably with your nearest competitor, you could be losing more business to them than is technically necessary. More and better content will even those odds.

Do you see the connection between content and results so far? Your content drives your online rankings and the more organized and effective you are in developing your content, the more people know about you and the more you can grow your audience.

Now, before everybody gets worried, remember that you don't have to do it all at once. I'm no Red Bull. But I've been steadily increasing my online presence over the years and I've now built up a pretty good set of resources as a result. But I had to start somewhere and I started with nothing!

So what does that do for me? Basically, my online content marketing strategy gives me a bigger online footprint than I as a small business might otherwise generate.

It also allows people to find out more about me, helps people see what working with me is like, shows my target audiences who I am and what I can do, helps educate people about how to improve their own writing, tells people that I'm available as a writer, editor, author and speaker and increases my credibility.

What's fun for me in working with my clients is watching their online garden grow – it takes time and effort but it's ultimately extremely satisfying.

Concept 2: Action – What do I have to do?

If you simply go back to your computer or device and search for the product or service you offer you'll get a sense of how well you Google. If you are not on the front page of the listings, it probably means you don't have a lot of content and you are not optimizing your content for searches (we'll get to that concept later).

The people who rank in the top spots for your category are not there by accident! They have an active content marketing strategy, which does not necessarily need to focus on the products and services they want people to buy – although it might do that as well — but rather does it focus on the issues and concerns of their audience.

Content is just that: it's the content of your online "real estate," all the words, images and videos you post to the internet that talk about the needs and problems of your ideal customers or clients. It positions you and your business as experts in your field. Your online "real estate holdings" are potentially unlimited but we are all limited as to how much time and energy we can spend on looking after all that property, so even though you COULD put details about your business up on hundreds of profile sites, you probably won't, at least in the beginning.

However much you can gracefully manage is the right amount.

According to the Content Marketing Institute, we're now living in a world where the non-media company has to become a media company. Their surveys show that large companies spend one in four marketing dollars on content marketing and that more than half will be increasing their spend over the next 12 months.

About one-third feel they're ineffective content marketers because they didn't know they were going to have to become journalists and writers and producers of content, and it's something they're not very familiar with. Most of the marketing managers surveyed said they're now spreading that content out over 17 or 18 different types of content.

For a small business in Canada or the US today, this might be information available on an array of sources, including: your website, your blog, your newsletter, your White Papers, your Linked In account, Facebook, Twitter, Slideshare, You Tube videos, podcasts, ezines, webinar series, Google Plus and Pinterest.

What is online that relates to you and your business and the interests of your potential customers? Is it enough to generate good search engine results?

Content Marketing Strategy Quickstart

Before you rush off to create a bunch of content, it's imperative that you spend some time developing a strategy first. You want to be clear on:

1. What your objectives are for your content marketing strategy

2. How you are going to measure success

3. Who your ideal customer is

4. What problems your business solves for them and

5. What content you could provide for them that would provide value and show you care

When you're clear on the answers to those questions, start setting some deadlines around your content production plans and enlist the assistance you need in order to make it happen.

I find that when people start looking at their content as a powerful tool rather than a mysterious expense they start to realize how valuable it is. A content marketing strategy will answer all of the answers above plus set out a schedule for adding to your existing content holdings at regular intervals. For example, I have my clients on a schedule where we write one blog post or one article weekly, we produce one Slideshare presentation a month, we post to our social media sites on a regular basis and we review our Google Analytics regularly so we know which pieces are generating the most interest; that allows us to fine tune our content to match visitor interest.

Concept 3:   Success – What Results Can You Expect?

My very first foray into content production, aside from my website of course, was my blog. I went to a social media marketing workshop and set up my Twitter, Linked In and Wordpress blog accounts, and I got very excited about this idea of a blog.

I'm a writer – a blog should be easy for me. And it more or less was. I hadn't been told how to develop an editorial schedule or to really target the needs of my clients and potential clients but I jumped in anyway and started writing about whatever struck my fancy. Low and behold, nothing happened. For six months.

I'd been told to stick with it and that a blog was not a fast path to cash but I think I could have generated more results faster if I'd been more strategic in the beginning with what I was saying and who I was targeting.

I had done no messaging, I had no editorial schedule and I had no calls to action. As I went along and learned that these were all important parts of the content creation continuum, I began to get more and better results.

I also didn't have a clue what Google analytics was, or how it might help me boost my efforts. I could spend a full day talking about Google Analytics and Tom Gray, the American internet marketing expert with whom I collaborate, could spend a whole month, I'm sure. It is very, very important. And it doesn't need to be scary.

Suffice to say that success with your content marketing strategy comes from three main factors:

Staying True to Your Brand

Being Consistent

Paying attention to your Google Analytics results

Ideally your content follows your branding. Once you know what your brand is and who your ideal audience is, you can take that information and embed it in all your content. You use it as a guide to write your website copy and absolutely everything else you write or anyone writes for you.

I work with a lot of businesses and not all of them have gone through a branding exercise so I often end up developing it for them. Now, I'm reasonably good at guessing but I can't be anywhere near as precise as a branding expert can be.

And here's what happens: I'll ask my client: "Who is your ideal client?"

And they'll say: "Everybody."

Well, it's hard to write to appeal to everybody. But I CAN write to a 35-year-old mother of twins who works full-time and has a husband who travels a lot and who has no spare time and a dwindling sense of excitement at what life was supposed to bring her.

Branding is very specific, detailed work and it allows you to be very targeted with your messaging. It's much better to get the right information to work with. If you haven't yet worked through the detailed exercises that help determine your brand identity, I highly recommend you invest in the process. It will ultimately save you time and money.

Especially when it comes to your content marketing strategy. Your brand identity will determine:

Who your ideal client is

What their major problems and concerns are

What you can do to solve their problems

What your ideal client's emotional "triggers" are likely to be

Where you need to price your products and services in order to maximize your appeal to your client

What kind of websites they tend to visit and/or what publications they tend to read

Your own brand will dictate the exact nature of your content marketing strategy, but let's talk generally for a moment here and take a big picture look at a strategy.

Obviously part of your strategy is going to be to have outstanding web content available on your website – your site itself is an example of content.

You also have the opportunity to express your brand and the promise inherent in working with you through your blog, your free downloads, your videos, ezines, YouTube, Facebook and Linked In.

They all need to be consistent with each other, and with your brand. How can you do that with, for example, a blog? You need an editorial outline.

Here's a sample of the one I use:

Your Target Client's biggest challenges

A third solution you can provide

Go ahead and complete a similar chart for your own business. You will end up with 15 solutions you provide and guess what? Each of these solutions now becomes the topic of a blog post, and if you blog once a week, that gives you four months worth of blog ideas.

Nothing kills credibility like a blog where there are five posts, the most recent of which was January of 2012. You need to keep at it! So, we have our editorial outline, now we need an editorial schedule: Jot down a number of deadline dates for developing your blog topic, completing your research, completing your final draft and posting your blog.

This will take 15 minutes of your time and I suggest you fill it in. Essentially, it's really easy to do this. You're going to take each of the 15 blog topics that you listed earlier and slot them into the left-hand column of the schedule. Everybody works differently and needs different amounts of time to craft a blog post but I tend to write three or four posts at once so the final drafts are all ready and waiting for me to get them up on my site.

Ideally you want to know ahead of time which blog is going up on your site on what date. And you're going to post each blog on the same day of the week. So start by writing in the dates when each of your 15 blogs is going to be posted.

Working backwards, how much time do you need to let a final draft "sit" before giving it a once-over prior to releasing it out into the public domain? If it's three days, then in the "Final Draft Complete By" column, work out when each blog will need to be completed in order to meet your posting deadlines, and enter those dates in that column.

And how long do you need a first draft to sit before finalizing it? (This may be affected by other factors, as well, such as the time you have available for editing, given other work-related commitments). If it's four days, then work out the dates for the first drafts of each of your 15 blog posts and enter them in the column stating "First Draft Complete by."

Finally, how much time do you need to allow between researching and writing the first draft of each blog?

Work out the dates that will give you enough breathing room and, again, enter those dates in the "Research Complete By" column.

And you're good to go – add these dates to your online calendar and you've got a set of moral deadlines to meet.

When you write your blog posts you want to make sure your content is clear, concise and easy to read. You want it to tell a story and you want it to resonate with your own voice. If you like to write you might want to write your blog posts yourself, but you can also hire a writer to help you out.

Now, how do you write a blog post? Some people break into a cold sweat at the idea of writing one and we're going to solve that problem right now with my handy dandy blog post writing template. And, actually, if you want a little more help with your writing generally, I invite you to read the other chapters in this book that deal with writing with clarity.

This is a template developed a number of years ago by a brilliant academic researcher by the name of Dr. Bernice McCarthy. She called it the '4Mat System' and it explains how people pay attention. While I've seen different numbers applied to different segments, the theory says basically that a certain percentage of the population wants to know "Why" something is important and if you'd don't satisfy their need for that information right away, they will tune out immediately and you will lose their attention.

Another segment of the population wants to know "What" the details of your program, project or event are, and although they will sit through the information about "Why" your program is important, they will disengage if they don't know what the details are next.

Other people like to know "How" something works. And, again, they will sit patiently through the "Why" and the "What" information but they need to know "How" your program works or they will tune you out.

And, finally, a certain percentage of the population wants to know what the implications of your program or service are and they will patiently review the why, what and how, but they feel dissatisfied unless you connect the dots to the implications for them so they can see how brilliant you are!

So, when I'm writing a blog post (and many other types of informational pieces) I arrange the information in that order to ensure I am providing all sectors of my audience the information they need the way they need it. This maximizes engagement and helps me stay structured.

I throw in an introductory sentence or paragraph, and a concluding sentence or paragraph, and I'm good to go.

I also end each blog post with a call to action such as this one:

"If you would like to know more about how I can help you achieve your goals while avoiding problems in all this, I invite you to contact me directly for more information at susan@crossmancommunications.com."

You want a call to action in everything you write so your audience knows what you expect of them. They don't have to do it. But at least you've made an option available for them.

A lot of people I coach are amazed at how easy it is to maintain a blog, you just have to get over that initial period where it is not a habit and it's not part of your day.

Now we've only looked at your blogging strategy and I think for most small businesses a blog should be the cornerstone of your content management strategy. You want to make sure your web content is strong and your writing is strong, and that all content revolves around your key messages and relates to your ideal audience. *And* that it is consistent across platforms.

As American writer Gene Fowler said, "Writing is easy. You just stare at a piece of paper until drops of blood form on your forehead." There is no shortcut to knitting the ideas together but if you find writing too hard to contemplate, again, hire a writer or consider creating either audio or video blog posts.

Now, we get to one of my favourite topics in the area of success with content, and that is Google Analytics.

One of the very important aspects of content marketing is that it is an extremely important way to boost your search engine rankings. There are people out there promoting the idea that you use massive amounts of verbiage to get you Googling well. But make no mistake: if the real human visitors to your site don't understand what you're telling them, then you won't make the sale. They'll bounce off your site faster than a superball.

Every person who has a website can have that website registered for free with Google Analytics. When you log into your account, you will be able to look at mountains of information about how many people have been coming to your website, what pages they viewed, how long they stayed, where they were online before they got to your site, what country they're from, what language they speak and on and on and on.

Why is that important? It's important because you can learn what parts of your content marketing strategy are working well and which ones need fine tuning just by looking at the Google Analytics information. If you have very few visitors to your site, and they are bouncing off almost as soon as they get there, then you probably need to beef up your other online properties and give people a compelling reason to visit your website and improve the content you have on the site itself.

If you have a lot of visitors to your site, and they are coming from a lot of other online locations, but your visitors bounce off your site on the home page, then you need to look at what you're offering and how well you're targeting your ideal clients. It's a very complex topic area and I feel it's worth hiring an internet marketing expert – like my friend Tom Gray in Denver – to help you maximize your online results. Of course, all of this is in aid of improving your search engine optimization (SEO) results, which feeds directly into your efforts to funnel visitors to your site.

Search Engine Optimization

I remember the wave of panic that hit me when I first came across the letters "SEO." I had no clue what they stood for and no idea why I should care. Even worse, I had a sinking feeling that they were probably terribly important. As a writer focused on staying competitive in an evolving business climate, I nervously jumped into the oceans of online information available on Search Engine Optimization. And although I'm still surfing the ever-evolving waves of change in this field, I've become a huge fan. It's an incredibly elegant business tool.

In simple terms, Search Engine Optimization (SEO) is a marketing strategy designed to help your organization rank at or near the top of the millions of listings that crop up when someone searches for what you have to offer. The closer you are to the top of the list, the more likely your perfect client is to click through to your website. It's an important strategy for success and other than paying for the time and energy of someone who knows what they're doing, it's all free.

Good SEO involves specific off- and on-site behaviors that work together around the effective use of "keywords " — terms your desired clients use when they are searching for what you offer. Finding the right keywords can take quite a bit of research, but they are crucial to successful SEO.

From an off-site perspective, you need as many links to your website as possible from other credible websites, and ideally the description of your organization on those off-site links will include language built around your keywords.

Your on-site strategy is a little more complicated as it involves much more finesse around such issues as the architecture of your site, the coding, the use of title tags (the words that show up in the bar running across the top of a web page) and last but not least, the content of your website itself.

The most important thing to remember is to use your keywords in everything you write. You need them in your headlines and you need them embedded in every page. They're there for one purpose only: to signal to the search engine "crawlers" the fact that your website is a perfect match for the keywords your ideal client just used to call up information from the internet.

The challenge is to write your content around your keywords in a way that engages the people reading it. While good SEO will generate visitor traffic, what happens when people get to your website is entirely up to you. If their experience is marred by poor writing or insufficient information, or if they're turned off by a ham-fisted display of nothing but keywords, then you've lost the chance to draw them more deeply into your marketing funnel. No engagement, no sale.

As SEO evolves, we're finding that engagement is by no means limited to the words you use either: in fact, information I obtained from Canada News Wire (CNW) shows that news releases that make use of photos, video and other forms of multimedia get a whopping 77% more views than those that use text alone. More views mean a greater possibility of converting those folks into customers and supporters. As an entrepreneur and avid student of this powerful marketing tool, I'm always on the lookout for ways to increase my market share. It took a lot of dedicated effort for me to learn what I needed to know in order to ensure my SEO and content strategies worked well together. And there's always more to learn. But once I got the hang of it, I never looked back.

Concept 4: Habits

So we've gained some clarity around Content Marketing, determined what Action to take and focused a little on how to be successful at this game. What habits do you need to cultivate in order to ensure your perfect clients make a beeline for your business?

As entrepreneurs, we're pulled in a million different directions in an average day and it can be difficult to guarantee that we have the time available to do all the things we need to do in order to be successful.

One of my clients was very excited about her content marketing strategy and she had worked very hard at getting it all organized and set up but the point at which I came into her life was the point where it had been two months since she had completed all her organizational work, and she hadn't written her first blog post yet.

This happens to a lot of people because, not surprisingly, it takes quite a bit of time and attention to develop content and make sure it gets to the appropriate place online. If you haven't been using a content marketing strategy and you aren't at a stage where you are ready to either hire a content marketing assistant or hire a consultant to look after it for you, it involves developing new habits.

From my observation, here are the top three habits entrepreneurs need to develop in order to succeed with content marketing:

Get in the habit of seeing your content marketing program as a high priority that adds a huge amount of value to your business. If you don't think it's important, you won't get to it. Remember when I said that I could trace 44% of my revenue last year to my online content marketing strategy? Would you like to increase your revenues by a similar amount over the next year? And if all that took was a little consistency, wouldn't that be worth the effort to make your content development a habit?

Put your content marketing deadlines in your calendar and work to those deadlines. I write three or four blog posts at a sitting, more if I can, so I know they're ready to go. I usually sit down and write my newsletter the day before the deadline but if I have to stay up until midnight to get it done, I do. People on my email list look forward very much to hearing what I have to say and I don't want to disappoint them or get them out of the habit of receiving my information.

Plus, I consider that as business owners, we exist to serve our clientele and one of the ways we can do that is to consistently provide quality content to people who need what we have to offer. I don't want to let people down!

Outsource as much of your content management as you can. Hire an assistant to post your blog to your website and to format and send out your newsletter. Hire someone to edit your blog posts and if you are not a writer, definitely hire someone to draft your white papers. While there's a little leeway in terms of professionalism in your blog posting, your white papers need to be top notch.

It can be hard for an entrepreneur to let go of the need to control every little detail and people often fear that hiring someone will dilute their "voice." It's a valid concern and I always recommend people hire the best talent they can afford in order to protect their reputation and further their business goals. That takes a fairly sophisticated business sense in itself but the right writer will have the skills and the desire to present you in the absolute best light possible.

A lot of behaviour that does not serve us well is the result of nothing more than a well-practiced habit. Sometimes we need to commit to *better* habits in order to create success and in the beginning that takes conscious effort.

As your business grows, you will have less time available to personally oversee your online content marketing strategy and that's when it makes sense to hire someone to look after it for you.

The beauty, however, is that the first-hand experience makes you sensitive to how you are being presented online and how you want to be, and you will be better able to manage a more junior person in the effort to continue building your business.

Content marketing is a very elegant system and, done well, it will help you stand out from your competition and generate dramatically more revenue. And no doubt other concepts are already on the horizon that will make content marketing one day obsolete. But for now, it's crucial that if you haven't already made the leap into content marketing, you do so as soon as you can, so you and your ideal customers can find each other in the delightful business of commercial transaction.

It's not that hard. And it works.

The road to hell is paved with adverbs.
— **Stephen King**

Here is a lesson in creative writing. First rule: Do not use semicolons. They are transvestite hermaphrodites representing absolutely nothing. All they do is show you've been to college.
— **Kurt Vonnegut**

Being a writer is a very peculiar sort of a job: it's always you versus a blank sheet of paper (or a blank screen) and quite often the blank piece of paper wins.
— **Neil Gaiman**

Make up a story... For our sake and yours forget your name in the street; tell us what the world has been to you in the dark places and in the light. Don't tell us what to believe, what to fear. Show us belief's wide skirt and the stitch that unravels fear's call.
— **Toni Morrison**

I never sit down to write. When I'm moved, I do it. I just wait for it to come. You just hear it. I can't really describe writing. It's in my head.
– **Lenny Kravitz**

This is how you do it: you sit down at the keyboard and you put one word after another until its done. It's that easy, and that hard.
— **Neil Gaiman**

Chapter 8: A Word on Fiction

While not everybody I've ever met has loved a good story I'd say many of the people I know have, at some point in their lives, enjoyed the telling of an enjoyable yarn. It's commonly understood that human beings have been telling stories around campfires for millennia and although our story telling media have changed over the generations, I think it's probably safe to say that the appreciation of a good story has not.

So why do people write — and read — fiction?

I think a big part of the answer lies in the human need for entertainment. Diving into an invented story is a wonderful way to escape our daily lives and try on a different world for a while.

Fiction takes us out of ourselves and into a place of wonder, delight, danger and mystery. It allows us to put down our fears, anxieties and problems for a while and get a break from the distracting worries that sometimes fill our days.

Writing fiction allows us to put ourselves in the driver's seat of collective imagination and help readers try on a world they might not, as yet, have imagined living.

It gives us the chance to put in front of our readers an alternate reality that might give them insights into the problems they themselves are facing and perhaps inspire a way of being that is more comfortable, fulfilling or enjoyable.

Fictional narrative is about tickling the fancy of readers in a way that non-fiction rarely can. I love a good biography as much as the next person. And while the lives of famous people are usually first-rate stories themselves, there's something delectable about the possibilities inherent in a story that is, for all intents and purposes, not the least bit true. And such stories help us to wonder, "Could it ever be?"

Fictional stories trigger the imagination in ways that non-fiction might not. They allow us to explore worlds that the three dimensions around us don't admit, to suspend the cold hard facts of our own reality and wander around in a world of "What if?"

Fiction allows us to dream, analyze, explain and understand our lives, and our purpose, in ways we hadn't yet considered. It can surprise us and it can bridge the gap between our own understanding of life and that of another person.

As either a writer or a reader of fictional stories, we can enjoy the experience of stretching the envelope of our existence to larger boundaries. And, quite often, stories are just plain fun. And who has too much fun anymore?

There's a special place on our shelves for fiction and although it's not everyone's cup of tea, I think it's safe to say that fiction, with its long history of survival in human society, is here to stay.

I meet many people who have reached a point in their lives where they can no longer keep their inner fiction writer trapped inside. Despite decades of more or less normal existence, they are driven to finally try their hand at creating a story and, if possible, to get it published.

I get so immersed in my work as a writer and an editor that I sometimes forget that not everyone knows the difference between fiction and non-fiction. So for anyone who scratches their head over that distinction, here it is:

A fictional story is about imaginary people, places or events. Novels and short stories are works of *fiction*.

A non-fiction book is about real people, places or events. Biographies and textbooks are examples of *non-fiction* books.

Aspects of a novel might seem real (indeed, the best writing of any sort tends to be believable) or it might be "based on a true story." Writers of fiction often spend countless hours researching the era in which they are setting their book, or the landscape in which the story unfolds. But the details of the story itself are invented.

We can get very technical describing the various parts of a novel and I've never been big on technicalities. If you're writing a novel yourself, you will probably want to become familiar with a few terms, however, so you have a handle on what you're doing.

When I wrote my first novel, "Shades of Teale," I didn't have a clue what I was doing: I jumped in and wrote the thing and had agonies of repair work to do after. This was all well and good but that might be part of the reason it took me 13 years to complete.

Let's save you some time, shall we, and look at what goes into a novel:

Plot is the unfolding of what happens in a novel and it usually revolves around what the character(s) do, say and think. There needs to be action in a novel in order to keep your readers engaged in your story. Your plot, sometimes referred to as your storyline, needs to unfold in a logical, orderly way so your readers don't get confused and put the book down in favour of other, more interesting activities like dusting the blinds or folding the laundry. Your plot has a beginning, a middle and an ending, and there may be lots of detours on the road between each point. Typically a character takes action, which is then followed by an emotional reaction and then a response. Plot is often depicted as an arc with a zig-zag line to represent the rise and fall of action. Plot also has a mid-level structure: scene and summary.

A lot of people make a lot of money teaching these details and while it's important to know about them, I think that it is just as important to be able to unleash your imagination and allow the story to develop as it will. Fiction writing is one of those rare occupations that require a certain amount of structure at the same as it requires unbridled imaginary abandon. It is creative and formulaic, to some extent, both at the same time. If you are new to the idea of writing fiction, I would like to suggest the most important work you will ever do lies in giving yourself permission to invent.

Exposition is the part of your story that provides the reader with important background information. Sometimes you need to provide some back-story that is not directly part of the action itself. If you're too wordy with it, you risk forcing your readers to tune out. To get around that, authors might use a flashback or have the character talk about his or thoughts of the past:

"When I was a child, I didn't realize that my family was unlike others."

Or the character might project some of the story into the future:

"It wasn't until I grew up that I realized we were different."

And speaking of characters...

We generally have at least two characters in a novel – the hero (back in high school he or she would have been called the protagonist) and the Hero's nemesis, who I would generally think of as the antagonist. The Hero drives the action of the story and we're really reading the story to find out about his or her adventure – be it physical, emotional or spiritual. While the hero may have numerous friends and supporters, he or she is brought into conflict with the antagonist – the person or group who does not want the hero to succeed. Ideally you want your hero's life to be miserable.

Readers love to see a hero struggle, and the more impossible you can make their journey, the more inspirational their success will be at the end. Bear in mind that the success doesn't mean they have to be alive at the end of the book (although I personally prefer happy endings), but rather that their goal or journey ideally needs to evince some level of triumph.

Readers generally like to see some sort of personal evolution in the characters in a novel, and you will keep people most engaged if you make your characters easy to visualize – describe their appearance and personality quirks, give them dialogue that allows them to express their deepest thoughts and feelings, make them move and make sure there are plenty of gestures: a raised eyebrow, a quiet smirk, a toss of the hair, a well-timed sneer. Don't forget to show your readers how your characters are feeling

Be Sure to Include Conflict

The more impossible the conflict is, the more interesting your novel will be. Sad to say, there is nothing more boring in a novel than a character whose life is in perfect order, whose relationships are all smooth and sunny and who has always loved their job. For pity's sake, give them flaws and weaknesses, enemies and inadequacies.

Show us the scheming uncle, the mean-spirited mother, the spouse with no backbone and the cousin who is out to take your character's meagre savings of. Engage us with drama and intrigue! Give yourself permission to say things that are not nice! That's what keeps us reading.

There have always been two sides to a story. Good and Evil. Make sure we know which one is which.

If there aren't any suitable characters to rage against, make sure your character has a good dose of conflict with someone or something. They can be pitted against Fate or God, Technology, Nature, the Supernatural, or even, God help us, themselves. Let's have fear and anxiety, insecurity and failure. It all makes for wonderful reading.

Symbolism

If you want to have fun with your story, be sure to use a little symbolism. There are reams of information available online about symbols and symbolism but to be honest, I don't think many of us want to be overwhelmed with it all the time. My favourite use of symbolism is subtle, gradual, so that I see the round table at which the lovers sit and think "Ahhh—Eternity!" But please don't give us all another black cat to ponder. That was probably old in Methuselah's time.

Foreshadowing

I think foreshadowing is a lovely technique for waking up the dark recesses of the brain and, again, it requires a gentle touch. If it's too obvious, your readers will know the end game before we're half way through, and if you're too ham-fisted it won't be fun to read what you've written. But subtle clues keep us on the edge of our seats, holding our breath, and wondering, "Was the author foreshadowing the character's death? Or not?" Give us the delight of not knowing!

Theme

I love working with themes and I quite often use them in my business writing, as well as in fiction. Ideally, a theme is like a quiet river of thought running underneath the texture of the words. A theme is a central idea or insight that unifies your story. Take "loyalty," for example. You might highlight the abuse of loyalty through the actions of one character and its desirability through the actions of another. It might be pure and sweet in the behaviour of a child and completely disregarded in the mind of a miserly grocer. But think about what you want to say about loyalty (or whatever theme you're playing with) and bring that commentary out through the interaction of your characters.

So how does one become a successful fiction writer?

The answer to that question could fill oceans.

Although some people might disagree, I am in the camp that says that becoming a good fiction writer stems from being a consistent reader. Read constantly and critically. Read for the joy of a good story and the lessons of an excellent writer. Somehow, in the process of reading, we absorb the conventions of writing and become experts in the field of what we like in a story and what we don't like. In observing other writers, we learn what we like and what we don't' like. My favourite authors include Stephen Leacock, Mark Twain and Charles Dickens. Those wonderful writers brought plenty of keen observation and painful irony to their work and the humour of their words, where it existed, has survived the relentless pounding of the years. For me, their work is timeless.

No matter which writers you favour, reading fiction helps expand the boundaries of your imagination. Writing is a creative process and there are those who believe that the output is closely related to the input. Read a lot and you will also find that the process of writing becomes easier. Reading a lot of crime fiction can help you understand what makes a crime thriller good. What elements need to be included and what absolutely must be absent? Trust your own judgement. And learn as much as you can about the process of writing in your genre.

I began my professional writing career more than three decades ago and I'm still learning. The field is limitless and the opportunity to evolve is endless. But practice is crucial. It allows us to experiment with fitting words together and it allows us to do it find ways to improve.

Theory and knowledge have their place, of course, but there is no substitute for practice. Ask any professional athlete or musician. Did they become virtuosos simply by knowing the theory of what they wanted to do? I think that 10,000 hours of practice gives us a big leg up.

My writing clients are all busy people. They have careers and families, charitable interests and big commitments. Most have had to make a decision to write their book No. Matter. What. It's challenging and it requires driving a massive stake in the ground and promising yourself you are going to make it happen. The amount of self-doubt that can accompany the decision to write a novel is immense. So the decision to write anyway, is an act of courage. If you are contemplating writing a novel, may I invite you to take a big breath and do it anyway – no matter what your mother, your partner, your friends or your inner demons have to say on the issue. You can do it if you decide you can.

It took me 13 years to finish my first novel. Thirteen years of a turbulent personal life that saw me the mother and step-mother of five children, and the doting owner of two wonderful dogs. I masterminded seven moves in 10 of those 13 years and I gave birth twice. I also walked my husband—who had been my high school sweetheart—to a traumatic death by stomach cancer. There were a lot of reasons not to finish my novel. It was a discouraging project that contributed not a penny to my family's well-being. I fully understand why people give up.

But what kept me going, aside from the encouragement of my family, was the thought that if I actually did give up I would never know if this was something I actually could do. It was my life's dream to become a published author, the icing on the cake of a successful career as a business writer. And it was a very scary goal.

But I think that success in any endeavour involves feeling the fear...and doing it anyway. No publisher will green light a half-finished manuscript. So if you're feeling the supreme discouragement of the exhausting challenge of writing your novel, ask yourself this: how many other would-be authors gave up and are now living out their lives wishing they hadn't given up on their dream? And how many successful authors started their writing careers feeling the exact same gripping fear of failure that you've been tripping on yourself? The difference between the successes and the failures is sometimes only the difference between wishing and deciding.

The amount of effort that goes into completing a work of fiction is monumental. Some of the authors whose work I have been privileged to edit thought they were done when they hired me to edit their manuscript. They had already invested countless hours in creating their opus, in making it the best they were capable of creating. That was me, too. When I sent my manuscript to my editor I had no clue there would still be so many errors to correct. After all, I had spent 13 years writing, re-writing, editing and agonizing over my characters and their stories.

I was a professional writer, for pity's sake! But my editor found areas where the motivation was unclear, the language was too wordy and she pinpointed areas where the details were missing. I laboured long and hard over that baby. And then I started over at the beginning.

There are some ego issues involved in working with an editor, by the way. Having someone else take a long hard look at your manuscript is like belly dancing on a busy street in your PJs. Every neurotic impulse you've ever had is on display, waiting for judgement. But being edited is not about you. It's about your book, it's about making that story the best it's possible for it to be.

Strong editing takes a good story and makes it incomparably better. Not everyone will love your finished, published book, by the way. Becoming a published author is a huge accomplishment that is sometimes met by catcalls and criticism. Don't take it personally! Learn from the experience, continue improving your writing skills, and stay true to your own inner voice, the one that says "This is the kind of writer I am." Not everyone is your perfect reader.

By the way, you could spend the next 10 years reading all the advice that's ever been written by writers who have been asked to share their insights on how to write fiction. It would all serve to keep you from writing, however, so my suggestion is that you absorb whatever you feel is important from the countless novels you've been reading, find a short primer on how to write fiction, and dive in.

You can learn as you go in this field and it's quite possible that the less you are guided by the experts, the more interesting your work will be. If you truly want to be published by a traditional publishing house, though, your finished product needs to be exemplary.

Fiction writing is a multi-layered, complex business. Who said there's only one way to do it right? The authors I've admired most are not the ones who had a formula figured out, but rather are they the people whose world view taught me something about my own humanity. Be that kind of person. Live, hurt, feel, think. Make mistakes, lose your temper.

Take us on your journey. Give us a piece of your heart and leak out the beatings of your soul. Honour your baggage and explore the many ways it's holding you back now. Or did, at one point.

Be humble and live your greatness. Ask questions for which you don't know the answers. Ignore the experts and ignore your loved ones when they tell you to give up before you get hurt.

Give yourself permission to bust out of the rules that surround you, and feel passionate about something. Anything.

Dream. Dare. Cry and eat chocolate until you feel sick. Take some chances and take some classes. Watch what's going on in the world around you and promise yourself that you will not forget how that feels.

Know what the rules are and then throw them away. Laugh. Love. Cringe. Become so immersed in the story of your own life that you become sensitive to the stories woven in the tapestry surrounding you.

Imagine. Fall. Tell the truth as you see it. And then shatter your own myths about who you are and who you are supposed to be. You can be whoever you choose to be. Make a choice.

Be the biggest you it's possible for you to be. And then help your characters do the same. They are aching to be unleashed. Can you free them? Only if you find a way to free that part of yourself that has been holding you back from your own success.

But most of all, share with us, your readers what you've learned about Life. We are waiting for what you are dreaming about sharing. Please hurry!

Just write every day of your life. Read intensely. Then see what happens. Most of my friends who are put on that diet have very pleasant careers.
— **Ray Bradbury**

Write the kind of story you would like to read. People will give you all sorts of advice about writing, but if you are not writing something you like, no one else will like it either.
— **Meg Cabot**

I haven't any right to criticize books, and I don't do it except when I hate them. I often want to criticize Jane Austen, but her books madden me so that I can't conceal my frenzy from the reader; and therefore I have to stop every time I begin. Every time I read Pride and Prejudice I want to dig her up and beat her over the skull with her own shin-bone.
— **Mark Twain**

Words do not express thoughts very well. They always become a little different immediately after they are expressed, a little distorted, a little foolish.
— **Hermann Hesse**

Don't bend; don't water it down; don't try to make it logical; don't edit your own soul according to the fashion. Rather, follow your most intense obsessions mercilessly.
— **Franz Kafka**

Chapter 9: The Magic of Marketing

The head of the marketing agency I wanted to work for leaned back in his chair and lit another cigarette. He squinted at me through the choking haze of smoke swirling around his head and he gave me a keen, appraising look. I had set up this interrogation weeks earlier when the agency's Vice-President told me I had passed the first round of interviews and it was up to The Boss to either green light or deep-six my application. We were only three minutes into the interview and already it wasn't looking good.

The Boss finally leaned forward in his chair and, still squinting, said nothing. I was reminded of Clint Eastwood in one of those cheesy old Western movies. Clint would squint mercilessly at the landscape, too, and then head out to gun down a whole town full of nasty characters. Although I was wearing, as I recall, a cream coloured suit with a pretty turquoise blouse, I wondered, for a moment, if I actually looked like someone of evil intent. This interview was not getting any better.

A massive cup of coffee balanced precariously on a tall and very messy stack of papers on the edge of The Boss's desk, and a jumbled bookshelf off to the left invited my attention. A gumball machine stood on a stand in one corner of the office and a heavy stressed leather jacket had been flung, artistically, almost, over the chair beside me. And still he said nothing.

I sat and looked around the room, pretending that this kind of silence between two strangers was a perfectly normal part of my professional career. I wondered what on Earth this guy was thinking. It was the verbal equivalent of waiting for someone to blink and I was determined not to be bullied into blinking. The Boss needed a copywriter. I was, at the very least, a writer, and I had experienced quite a lot of success in my field, up until that very brittle moment in time.

Fresh from a year off as a new mother, I was looking for a job that did not require a lengthy commute and I figured, in the cocky way of the very young, that I could do anything. Even write marketing copy. Even without any experience. Even without any training.

How hard could it be?

I leaned back comfortably in my own chair and crossed my ankles, as I had been taught to do as a young girl. I casually leaned down and tugged my portfolio out of the battered briefcase I had dug out of the bottom of a closet, and I set the accordion file containing my clips on the only corner of the desk that had not been attacked by the kind of creeping clutter that begs for professional attention. I waited. He waited.

Finally, after what seemed like enough time to finish seven innings of an average baseball game, the great man spoke.

"So?" he said.

"So?" I repeated. It would have been nice if he could smile, and I thought he might have quite a nice face if he ever deigned to wrestle it into a cheerful expression. As it was, he looked dour and critical. He had a beard and a mustache, hair down to his shirt collar and gray-blue eyes that were framed by exceedingly long eyelashes. He was tall and lanky. Graceful. Possibly sleep deprived. What on Earth did this man want?

"So you say you're a writer." It was a question. Not a very nice one.

"I *am* a writer," I said archly. He instructed me to pull out my best clips and I did. Feature articles from the London Free Press, a daily newspaper. Feature articles from Canadian Press, the nation's newswire service. Press releases, speeches and media backgrounders from the Ontario Ministry of Health, THE largest provincial ministry. In. All. Of. Canada. One after another I pulled them out of my file and pushed them across the desk for his review.

After approximately 184 seconds he looked at me and snarled.

"What is this crap?" he asked. My heart sank. It was the best I could do, in point of fact, and plenty of people had told me it was great stuff.

My introduction to marketing was less than stellar. But I got the job anyway. What followed was three years of metaphorical head-banging and actual hand-wringing, loud arguments and quiet consolations, discussions, explanations, frustrations and breakthroughs as I teased out of my reluctant mentor the strategies and techniques that were to turn me into a solid marketing copywriter. He patently did not want to teach me. But I was the best he had found and, dad gummit, he was going to work with me.

The problem, dear readers, is that writing marketing copy is nothing like writing news articles or press releases or briefing notes. Those communication vehicles require, more or less, little more than the solid recitation of factual information. They require great research and interview skills, a nice way with people, a solid sense of how to organize information and a terrific command of the written language. A little wide-eyed guile doesn't hurt. And a plan is essential. It's not that it's easy to do all of the above. It's just that it's much easier than writing hard core marketing copy.

There were many times during my marketing apprenticeship all those years ago when I felt my heart tackled by terror and my legs gripped by a strong urge to run. Was I ever going to figure this out? On many panicked mornings, as I drove to the office, it seemed unlikely. And I did. Finally.

It would have helped to have had a little context from which to work and so I'll pass along to you my favourite definition of marketing. Actually, it's my own definition, and one I developed after the umpteenth person asked me, "So, what is marketing, anyway? I would love to help you avoid some of the struggle I experienced before I landed on this key piece of information. Marketing seems to be a monolithic topic, full of mystery and mayhem, and it is certainly a vast subject area that one could spend decades exploring. Some people do.

But at its heart, marketing is quite simple: it encompasses all of the activities you need to do in order to start conversations with people who are likely to buy from you. Like create a website, a Linked In profile, a You Tube video or a direct mail piece. Or maybe launch an email marketing or pay per click campaign, deliver a speech, write a blog or send out a newsletter. The possibilities are endless and most of them require you to write something.

Writing strong marketing copy requires you to give up any illusion you have ever had about what is important in the world. Because most of us assume that what's important to us is important to other people as well. We think that we need to send our potential customers avalanches of information that tell them how amazing we are.

When you're writing your web content, or any marketing material, really, you rarely want to write about how great you are. Because your perfect client doesn't really want to hear about you. Your perfect client wants to hear words that demonstrate how well you understand the agony he or she is going through in getting through just one more day of their lives without the assistance you can provide. They want to know that you understand, down to the smallest detail, how much they are suffering. They want a ray of hope in a bleak world.

But first of all you have to know who "they" are.

Rule number one in writing your web and other marketing content is to figure out who is going to buy what you're selling.

The answer is not "everybody." Nor is it "anybody." Out there, somewhere, is a demographic of individuals who are the perfect recipients of what you have to offer. And the more narrowly you can define them, the easier it is to get them to flock to your product or service. Trust me on this one.

You want to know things like how old they are, what they do in life, what kind of car they drive and how old it is. Automatic or standard transmission? Maybe they prefer public transit because it's better for the environment. Do they have kids or grandchildren, a university education or a desire to improve the world? The more you know about your perfect customer, the more you can address their problems.

Which is where the pain part comes in.

What keeps them up at night? How are they suffering? What do they want more of or less of? What makes them crazy and what makes their heart sing? You want to crawl inside the skin of your perfect customer and wear their lives so you know, really *know*, down at the drooling, bended knee pit of their worst day, how you can help them get back on the fast track, where they really belong.

And what *can* you do to help?

While you're lying on your belly on the floor beside your perfect customer, and they are stifling whimpers of frustration as they manfully pretend there is nothing wrong, you want to gently, very gently, paint for them a picture of how you can help their miserable wind-sucking problem disappear into thin air so you can transform their world into a complete masterpiece of comfort and delight.

Of course you are never, Ever going to lie to anyone in your web copy. Always Tell the Truth. Which requires a little work on your part because you need to figure out what the Truth actually is, and that's why you need to go through an in-depth branding exercise before you even consider writing your own web copy.

What is your Truth?

You need to find out what it is you do that no one else can do, and for this you need to go through a branding process. This is a microbial course of discovery in action that many entrepreneurs and business people sidestep because it is so much bloody darned work. It requires a level of self-analysis that borders on therapy. It is time-consuming and, if you do it with the assistance of a branding expert, it does cost money.

And it is worth every dime. Knowing the ins and outs of your brand delivers a wealth of information that is exceedingly useful in developing your web or other marketing copy. What do you offer and why is it better? Who do you serve and how do you serve them? What are your competitive advantages? What are you less adept at delivering? What promises do you and your brand make to your customers and clients? How much do you charge? And so much more!

If you're hiring a copywriter, you can hand all of that written, codified branding information over to him or her and avoid the need for in-depth interviews or time-consuming telephone conversations that might start with the lurching, painstaking question, "So…what exactly do you *do*?" Your branding documentation explains the whole schmeer in minute detail and gives your copywriter (and your graphic designer, by the way), a lot of priceless information that can help them present you precisely the way you need to be portrayed.

As a copywriter with years of experience and a mountain of exclusive training behind me, I can make highly educated and extremely intelligent guesses about what your brand might be. I'm right a great percentage of the time. But do you really want to leave the definition of your business over to someone who is not you? What if you chance to hire a writer who *doesn't* have the scars, bruises and haggard appearance that summarize a life of learning marketing the hard way? What if they are full of confidence and bravado, and sit before you with clean fingernails and a collection of really great bohemian scarves...only to tell you they think it would be a great idea to highlight your previous experience job experience on the Home page of your website?

There might be times when that's a great idea. But generally, NO! Don't do it!

Talk about your perfect client's biggest challenges. And mention how you can make their life better.

Technicalities

There's a lot of technical information available on the web that is about as captivating to read as a university text book. And some very smart people get paid enormous amounts of money to research, analyze and quantify marketing information for those very same textbooks. There is a place for that. But most small business owners are light on their feet and low to the ground. They don't have a lot of time to spend on anything other than revenue generating activities. They want the straight goods and they want to know where to spend their time and money so they get the biggest bang for the buck.

So what are the straight goods of marketing copywriting? Aside from the points we've covered above (and elsewhere in this book), here's what I've learned:

Use great headlines. They keep people reading.

Numbers work well (e.g. "The Five Expert Secrets of Writing to Sell")

Action words are good, too (e.g. "Supercharge Your Sales!")

Words that speak to results are effective (e.g. "Double Your Revenue in Three Months or Less")

And ask questions (e.g. "Are These Writing Mistakes Costing You Money?")

There is currently some debate as to whether it's a good idea to use your keywords in headlines and I fall into the camp that stands in the middle of the internet playground wondering, "Well, why *wouldn't* I use keywords in a headline, if I can do it with finesse?"

Keep it short. Especially on the web. Statistics say you have anywhere from three to nine seconds to grab and hold a reader's attention so don't waste a single one. Use short, simple words, rather than fancy ones, vary the length of your sentences and include numbered lists or bullet points for maximum impact. You aren't out to impress people with your vocabulary here. You are attempting to start conversations with the people who might want to buy what you are selling.

Put your most important information up front. Most readers are not going to stick around to the end of your web page, although some do. If you're offering special pricing on an item for this week only, tell your readers sooner, rather than later, and make sure you stress *why* your product or service is important to your readers.

Stress the benefits of what you offer. It's nice that you're selling a pen that doesn't leak but what's going to matter to me, the reader, is what's in it for me. I'm a lazy thinker sometimes so connect the dots for me. Sure, tell me the pen doesn't leak but also point out that, as a result, I never again need to deal with inky and potentially embarrassing messes in my laptop bag or jeans pocket.

Use Active Voice. Rather than tell me that "items broken during delivery will be returned to the manufacturer by our staff" say "our staff will return all items broken during delivery to the manufacturer." When you were in grade school, you might have seen that one expressed as "The dog was walked by the boy." It would be turned into "The boy walked the dog." Active voice represents a much more efficient use of words than passive voice, and it gets the point across much faster and with greater impact.

Use positive words instead of negative ones. "We want you to enjoy the benefits of lower payments" glides into the hearts of your readers so much more easily than "We don't want you to struggle with high payments."

Be assertive. Stand up for your greatness. A statement: "We try to do our best on every project we undertake" doesn't build confidence. But, "We aim to outperform the competition on every project we undertake," gets attention!

Be specific. It's great to hear that your product or service helped many consumers or businesspeople succeed last year. But I'll be more convinced if you tell me how many people you affected, and how your efforts increased their success. Did their revenues or savings increase by an average of 29%? Did you help them increase their customer base by an average of 18%? Did they notice a drop in complaints from customers or family members of at least 27% because of what you did? Give me the details!

Engage the senses! Embed words in your copy that give audio, visual and kinesthetic depth to your language. Is your product colourful, shiny, glossy or beautiful? Can people hear the words of praise their partners will be heaping on them when they show off their latest purchase from your establishment? Will they feel an intense pride of ownership or a heady thrill of achievement because of something you've sold to them? What emotional vibrancy can you include in your copy? Sense-oriented words rock the world of your reader – engage them!

Avoid jargon. Your field may be rife with pet terms that people "in-the-know" fling at each other with confident abandon. But your ideal customer might not know what those terms are, and there's a good chance they will tune out if they hear them and feel confused.

Go easy on the adjectives. I love an adjective as much as the next writer but I have to tone it down when I'm writing marketing copy. *And* when I'm writing fiction, oddly enough. Come to think of it, it's a good idea to use adjectives sparingly in almost all the writing you do, fun as they are. Adjectives—words that describes things—detract from the masterful train of effectiveness that you're trying to create with your language. But if you want to add some rocket fuel to your writing style, latch onto a horde of powerful verbs (action words) and see what happens.

Tell a story. Everybody loves a story. It doesn't have to be a long one and it doesn't have to be on your home page. If there is something unique about how you came to be in business, and if it ties in with your commitment to quality products and services, tell your readers about that. It helps position you as a real human being and will capture our imagination in a way that facts and figures will not.

Use metaphors. Dr. Gerald Zaltman and Dr. Lindsay Zaltman of Harvard University did extensive marketing research a few years ago and determined that seven metaphors consistently increase buying behaviour in people living in pretty well every country in the world. And I haven't heard a single other copywriter talking about this! So be the first businessperson on your block to scoop the competition. When you write your marketing copy, include information on: Balance, Journeys, Transformations, Containers, Connections, Resources and Control.

Include a call to action. A visitor has arrived on your site, read your headline and scrolled to the bottom of Page One. What is it you want them to do next? Download your free report? View your weekly specials? Call for a free consultation? If you want to keep the conversation going (and you do!) make it easy for readers to take the next step: but tell them what it is first.

Include some testimonials or third-party endorsements. But leave it open-ended. Some people don't care what other people think of your product or service—they want to decide for themselves whether you're any good at what you do, and you want to respectfully invite them to do that. So while you might include a quote from a satisfied customer on the one hand, make sure you add in a comment that says, "But you probably want to check it out for yourself and we'd be pleased to answer any questions you have about the effectiveness of our product."

Avoid grammatical mistakes. Always proof your marketing copy and have someone else read it *before* you go live with it. Typos, spelling mistakes, confusing sentences, and the like, all damage your credibility and—whether you like it or not— they call your professionalism into question. My favourite grammatical reference book is still the Strunk and White classic, "The Elements of Style." You can get a paperback edition on amazon.com for a few dollars or access the online version for free at www.bartleby.com.

Use images. People love pictures, and so do the search engines. One well-placed optimized image of an idea or feeling you would like to convey is still worth 1,000 words.

So what do you think? Does that help? Don't be discouraged if this seems daunting at first. Although there is a knack to writing marketing copy it all pretty much turns on whether you know who your perfect customer is, what they need and what you can do to make their life better.

The man who first taught me the tricks of the copywriting trade was a reluctant teacher at best. He was memorable, however, and his image has stuck with me for decades now, as have many of the others who've had a part in my development as a writer. Perhaps the best advice The Boss gave me, however, occurred late one evening as we raced to meet yet another impossible deadline. It was the simplest piece of advice imaginable. And it was very, very powerful.

The Boss was tired of giving me detailed directions about phrasing and creativity, colour and benefits. He was tired of my technical questions and my inability to read his mind. He just wanted me to get it.

So he sat at his desk with his cigarette cradled in his right hand and his favourite pen balanced in his left. He leaned back in his chair and glanced thankfully at the can of beer he had parked neatly beside his ash tray. He sighed heavily and looked up at the ceiling for a long time, as though asking for just a little more patience, a little more time.

"None of that other stuff matters all that much, Susie," he said finally. "Ya just gotta make it *cook*."

So I did.

The Boss is gone, now, the victim of a heart attack that occurred some years before one might have expected him to leave us. But between the spark of the future and the dust of the ages, his advice lingers: Go ahead, readers. Make it *cook*.

When asked, "How do you write?" I invariably answer, "One word at a time," and the answer is invariably dismissed. But that is all it is. It sounds too simple to be true, but consider the Great Wall of China, if you will: one stone at a time, man. That's all. One stone at a time. But I've read you can see that motherfucker from space without a telescope.
— **Stephen King**

Great writers are indecent people
they live unfairly
saving the best part for paper.
good human beings save the world
so that bastards like me can keep creating art,
become immortal.
if you read this after I am dead
it means I made it.
— **Charles Bukowski**

There is such a place as fairyland – but only children can find the way to it. And they do not know that it is fairyland until they have grown so old that they forget the way. One bitter day, when they seek it and cannot find it, they realize what they have lost; and that is the tragedy of life. On that day the gates of Eden are shut behind them and the age of gold is over. Henceforth they must dwell in the common light of common day. Only a few, who remain children at heart, can ever find that fair, lost path again; and blessed are they above mortals. They, and only they, can bring us tidings from that dear country where we once sojourned and from which we must evermore be exiles. The world calls them its singers and poets and artists and story-tellers; but they are just people who have never forgotten the way to fairyland.
— **L.M. Montgomery**

It has often been said
there's so much to be read,
you never can cram
all those words in your head.

So the writer who breeds
more words than he needs
is making a chore
for the reader who reads.

That's why my belief is
the briefer the brief is,
the greater the sigh
of the reader's relief is.

And that's why your books
have such power and strength.
You publish with shorth!
(Shorth is better than length.)
— Dr. Seuss

In many cases when a reader puts a story aside because it 'got boring,' the boredom arose because the writer grew enchanted with his powers of description and lost sight of his priority, which is to keep the ball rolling.
— Stephen King

We write, not with the fingers, but with the whole person. The nerve, which controls the pen winds itself about every fibre of our being, threads the heart, pierces the liver.
— Virginia Woolf

Chapter 10: Concluding Thoughts

"You'll never get a job in journalism without a Master's degree," my University professor said with finality. "Can't be done anymore." It was February of my last year at Queen's University and the question of the Rest of My Life was looming large, lurking dangerously on the other side of final exams. I was still mired in the panic of completing what seemed like an endless list of essay papers required for my degree in Political Studies and I was contributing plenty of articles, and taking part in three press nights a week, as an enthusiastic member of the Queen's Journal, the university's student newspaper.

My professor's words curdled in my heart. He was teaching a 'Politics and the Media' course I was taking and I had gone to him for advice on how to land that perfect job in journalism. I just knew it was out there waiting for me. I had wanted to be a news reporter for years and had even chosen my field of study on the basis of what would prepare me best for a career in print journalism. Political Studies, of course — doesn't almost everything come down to politics? Well, I thought so at the time. What my prof had to say couldn't possibly be true. But he was adamant.

"You can do it at Western or Carleton," he said.

I slumped away from our conversation in despair. I couldn't afford another degree. It was the height of the '82 Recession and my father was self-employed. We had managed my undergrad expenses but there was no way another degree was going to fit into the plan. I had to find another way.

In the end, the question of my career was answered by my mother's massive stroke, the news of which I received just as I was about to write my first final exam in April that year. I raced home to the London area to keep watch with my family and, after Mom was out of danger, somehow managed to return to Kingston to complete my other exams. The year that followed was a difficult one for my family. At the time we lived on a beautiful 18-acre country property in an ancient farmhouse that my mother had been in the process of renovating. She had done a beautiful job but there was still some work to be done. With Dad running a business, Mom needing intensive therapy and assistance, and the house and property needing constant upkeep, I elected to stay home and look after things. My friends headed off to grad school or great jobs, or extended travels in Europe, and I became swept up in the intense task of looking after a family and a home.

I thought wryly back to the conversation my prof and I had had about my career in journalism. "What career?" I wondered, at times. But never one to give up, I started scouting for opportunities. Journalists were losing their jobs left, right and centre at the time, victims of the drop in ad revenue the Recession had engendered. I landed some ongoing freelance work with a small weekly paper and managed my assignments for "Western Ontario Business," around my mother's therapy. I sweetly harassed the Managing Editor of the London Free Press until he agreed to give me a four-hour evening shift in the newsroom that was traditionally reserved for the Master of Journalism students at the University of Western Ontario. I worked part-time for my father whenever I could spare the time. And I took flying lessons.

After a year my mother's condition was much improved and my father encouraged me to move out. My four-hour shift at the Freeps had turned into full-time contract work as a Homes/Features writer — a maternity replacement. There was no telling what would happen when the writer I was replacing returned to work so I started looking for another post. Canadian Press in Toronto gave me a junior position for minimal pay and I snapped it up. In time I was offered a position as a media relations officer for the Ontario Ministry of Health for twice what I was earning at CP. And no night shifts.

After several years there I took time out for an extended adventure in England with my first husband and returned home after a couple of years with a new baby. With my marriage on the rocks, I went to work as a marketing copywriter for a marketing agency. The head of the agency looked at the samples I showed him from my portfolio and snarled.

"What is this garbage?" he barked. I had been racked up almost seven years of professional experience by that point. What was he talking about? In the end I realized that he was talking about the difference between journalism, PR and marketing. Marketing is not about reciting information. It's about influencing behaviour. There is a huge difference, and it's not something that I had ever been taught. Although the fellow thought I had promise, he made it clear I had to learn how to write "properly" and he was definitely not going to teach me. I was back on a learning curve, and it was not an easy one. After a year or two I was getting glowing reports and two years later I left to make a living as a freelance writer. I haven't had a steady job since.

What I have had, however, is a lot of insight into this business of writing for a living. At every turn of the wheel

I've had to gain new skills applicable to a new way of writing. It hasn't always been easy but I have always been prepared to start at the bottom and work my way up. I've always been determined to learn, to grow, to improve. My professor might have been right, all those years ago, when he told me I needed a degree in journalism. I might well have landed a great job immediately upon graduation and maintained employment consistently all the way along in a field that even today does not seem too promising. We will never know. And certainly, my career trajectory has not been what I ever imagined it would be. Surprises have jumped out from almost every corner, some delightful and some not so much.

But the advice I give to young people just starting out on a writing career is much different from the advice I received: "If this is what you really want to do," I say, "then go for it. Get as much training, experience and education as you can possibly cram into your life, and be willing to contribute every ounce of energy you have to the attainment of your goal. You will either find a way to make it work or not, and either way, I believe the Universe has your back."

For people who simply want to write better and with less stress, my advice is usually somewhat different. "Don't be too hard on yourself," I say. "Writing is a skill that can be learned. If this is something you really want to do, get as much training, experience and education as you can possibly cram into your life. Oh, and read. A lot."

Whatever category you fall into, I wish you well in all your endeavours and I hope your travels are all happy ones. Best wishes for success on all fronts.

Susan Crossman

About the Author

Susan Crossman is a writer, author, editor and speaker who was born in Dryden, Ontario, towards the tail end of the Baby Boom. She spent her early years among the rocks, lakes and trees of the Canadian Shield and moved with her family to London, Ontario, at age six. She resided there almost continuously until leaving for Kingston and Queen's University at age 19.

Since then she has lived in Toronto, Montreal and London, England, and has travelled extensively and whenever possible throughout North America, Europe and Asia.

While the core of Susan's writing activities surround the development of web content for businesses and the editing of manuscripts for other authors, she has written several books, including **The Write Way**; the novel, **Shades of Teale,** which tells the story of a woman's journey through an unhappy marriage, and **Passages to Epiphany,** a collection of non-fiction stories relating eye-opening experiences during her life as a writer, mother, widow, seeker and traveller.

Susan has an M.A. degree in English Literature and she is a certified General and Master Practitioner of neuro-linguistic programming (NLP). She is a licensed private pilot and a certified Awakening Coach and she is adept at search engine optimization (SEO) and social media marketing (SMM); she is proficient in issues around the Enneagram system of personality profiling and she speaks five languages (three well). For more information about Susan's business and creative writing, visit www.crossmancommunications.com

Manor House Publishing
www.manor-house.biz
905-648-2193